PRISONERS AND PARTISANS:
ESCAPE AND EVASION
IN WORLD WAR II ITALY

MALCOLM TUDOR, BSc.

EMILIA PUBLISHING

ISBN (13) 978-0-9538964-3-1
ISBN (10) 0-9538964-3-9

The author with former partisans of the Valdarda at Teruzzi di
Morfasso: (left to right) Mino Avogadri, Oreste Scaglioni,
Malcolm Tudor and Luigi Sesenna.

First published in 2006 by

EMILIA PUBLISHING
Woodlands, Bryn Gardens,
Newtown, Powys, SY16 2DR
United Kingdom

www.emiliapublishing.com

To the memory of my parents:

Kenneth Winston Tudor

Quartermaster Sergeant, Royal Corps of Signals,
France, North Africa, Sicily,
Italy and Austria

and

Clara Elvira Maria Tudor (née Dall' Arda)

'At the Italian Armistice it would have been very easy to "keep your head down" and out of the way. Your mother chose the more dangerous course of helping those she could whatever the risk. Thousands of us were helped, fed and hidden by those Italians who chose the hard and dangerous way. So many of us owed our lives to them. The Monte San Martino Trust will continue to record and remember thousands of Italians like your mother.'

- Uff. Cav. J Keith Killby, OBE, founder of the Monte San Martino Trust.

The Piacentine Apennines at Rabbini di Monastero, Morfasso.
(Cordani)

CONTENTS

Other books by Malcolm Tudor:

'British Prisoners of War in Italy: Paths to Freedom'

'Escape from Italy, 1943-45'

'Special Force: SOE and the Italian Resistance
1943-1945'

Also available from Emilia Publishing

ACKNOWLEDGEMENTS

I would like to thank veterans of the campaign and
relatives who have provided me with information.
Specific credits appear in the appropriate chapters.

Photographs kindly contributed by:

Richard Bryson, Rosemary Clarke,
Andrea Cordani and Cris Kydd.

- Other images are from my collection -

1 *ARMISTIZIO*

In its thirty-eighth month as an ally of Germany in the Second World War the Kingdom of Italy surrendered to Allied Forces. On the evening of Wednesday, 8 September 1943, the head of the Italian Government, Marshal Pietro Badoglio, said in a radio broadcast:

> Italy has been compelled to withdraw from the unequal struggle ... Hostilities by Italian Forces against the Anglo-Americans will now cease on every front. However, our forces will respond to possible attacks from any other quarter.

The London *News Chronicle* reported next day:

> At 5.30 last night General Eisenhower, Allied C-in-C in the Mediterranean, announced: 'The Italian Government has surrendered its armed forces unconditionally. As Allied Commander-in-Chief, I have granted a military armistice, the terms of which have been approved by the governments of the United Kingdom, the United States and the Union of Soviet Socialist Republics.'

The Instrument of Armistice and Surrender of the Italian Forces to General Eisenhower had been signed on Friday, 3 September in an olive grove at Cassibile in Sicily. Marshal Badoglio was represented by Brigadier General Giuseppe Castellano and General Eisenhower by his Chief of Staff, Major General Walter Bedell Smith. Before dawn, the British Eighth Army had crossed the Straits of Messina to the Italian mainland.

The ceremony remained secret. The conditions of the Armistice were not to be made public without the prior approval of the Allied Commander-in-Chief. The Italian Government undertook to proclaim the agreement once he had made the announcement, but their insistence that this should follow the main Allied landing had been firmly rejected by Major General Bedell Smith on 31 August.

The dramatic events of the subsequent days are nicely summarised by Winston Churchill in his history, *The Second World War*:

1

It now remained to coordinate the terms of the Italian surrender with our military strategy. The American General Taylor, of the 82nd Airborne Division, was sent to Rome on 7 September. His secret mission was to arrange with the Italian General Staff for the airfields around the capital to be seized during the night of the 9th. But the situation had radically changed since Castellano had asked for Allied protection. The Germans had powerful forces at hand and appeared to be in possession of the airfields. The Italian Army was demoralised and short of ammunition. Divided counsels seethed round Badoglio. Taylor demanded to see him. Everything hung in the balance. The Italian leaders now feared that any announcement of the surrender, which had already been signed, would lead to the immediate German occupation of Rome and the end of the Badoglio Government. At two o' clock on the morning of 8 September General Taylor saw Badoglio, who, since the airfields were lost, begged for delay in broadcasting the Armistice terms. He had in fact already telegraphed to Algiers that the security of the Rome airfields could not be guaranteed. The air descent was therefore cancelled. [1]

The main Anglo-American landing at Salerno, codenamed Avalanche, was due to take place within 24 hours. An angry General Eisenhower telegraphed the Joint Chiefs of Staff:

I have just completed a conference with the principal commanders and have determined *not* to accept the Italian change of attitude. We intend to proceed in accordance with plan for the announcement of the armistice and with subsequent propaganda and other measures. Marshal Badoglio is being informed through our direct link that this instrument entered into by his accredited representative with presumed good faith on both sides is considered valid and binding and that we will *not* recognise any deviation from our original agreement.

The 'direct link' was a British Special Operations Executive (SOE) agent. Between 30 August and 8 September Lieutenant Richard Mallaby exchanged 70 messages with Eisenhower's HQ from the top floor of the Italian High Command building in Rome.

In a joint message to the general, President Roosevelt and Prime Minister Churchill told him: 'The agreement having been signed, you should make such public announcement regarding it as would facilitate your military operations.'

At 6pm on Wednesday, 8 September, General Eisenhower made the announcement of the Armistice. As agreed at Cassibile, Marshal Badoglio's statement followed an hour later from Rome. The broadcast was not live, but a gramophone recording. Churchill wrote: 'The surrender of Italy had been completed.'

The Germans began the encirclement of the capital. In the early hours of Thursday, 9 September, a convoy of five cars left through the eastern gates for the Adriatic port of Pescara. On board were the Royal Family, the heads of the army and navy, Marshal Badoglio, a few ministers and Lieutenant Mallaby. Two corvettes carried the party to Brindisi. They arrived early on Friday, the 10th. The lieutenant was awarded an immediate Military Cross.

A royalist government was created in liberated territory in the south. The Germans occupied the remaining 80 per cent of the country and freed the former dictator, Benito Mussolini, on 12 September. He was installed as head of the *Repubblica Sociale Italiana* (RSI), or Italian Social Republic, with its headquarters at Salò on Lake Garda.

On 13 October, the Royal Italian Government declared war on Germany. Great Britain, the United States and the Soviet Union accorded Italy the status of co-belligerent.

'Avalanche' was successful and on 16 September the 5th and 8th armies linked up 40 miles south of the bridgehead. The Germans eventually pulled back to the winter Gustav Line between Minturno on the Tyrrhenian Sea and Ortona on the Adriatic. Central Italy was not to be liberated until the following summer and the north only in May 1945. What of the Allied prisoners of war (POWs) in Italy?

The third condition of the Armistice stated that: 'All prisoners or internees of the United Nations are to be immediately turned over to the Allied Commander-in-Chief, and none of these may now or at any time be evacuated to Germany.'

An order from the Italian War Office to their camp commandants on 6 September said:

British POWs - Prevent them falling into German hands.
In the event that it is not possible to defend efficiently all

3

the camps, set at liberty all the white prisoners but keep the blacks in prison.

Facilitate their escape either to Switzerland or along the Adriatic coast to southern Italy. Labour units in civilian clothes may also be helped, provided they are away from the German line of retreat. At the opportune moment the freed prisoners should be given reserve rations and directions as to which route they should follow.

A British blueprint for dealing with the rescue and repatriation of Allied prisoners of war in the probable event of an Italian surrender had been settled as early as March 1943. The plan was straightforward. The military terms of an armistice with the Italian Government would include instructions to release the POWs and prevent them being transported to Germany. To administer liberated territory an Armistice Commission would be required. It would appoint a Prisoner of War Sub Commission. To deal with the number of Allied servicemen held in Italy a headquarters and field staff of over 6,000 would be necessary. They would take over the camps and the inmates would gradually be moved to collection points and on to transit camps capable of holding four to five thousand men each. The centres would be created near the ports of embarkation: Genoa, Leghorn, Naples and Brindisi.

The plan envisaged Allied control of Italian territory and depended upon the prisoners remaining in their camps. A brief message to this effect was sent to the Senior British Officer (SBO) or his equivalent in all the camps in Italy using MI 9's usual secret channels of coded letters and radio messages. The instruction, dated 7 June, would become notorious as the 'stand fast order.'

A paper to the twenty-sixth Imperial Prisoners of War Committee Meeting held in London on the actual day of the announcement of the Armistice stated:

It is not known whether on the signing of the Armistice with Italy, the whole country or certain strategic points only will be occupied by Allied troops. If, however, the Badoglio Government were to conclude an Armistice the Germans might be able to profit by the confusion in order to seize some prisoners whose fate in this regard would depend on whether they were north or south of the line on which the Germans decided to stand.

4

News of the Armistice arrived at the camps across Italy in the evening. The Italian commandants with few exceptions attempted to carry out their orders to safeguard the prisoners and if necessary ensure their release to prevent them falling into German hands. Next morning, Senior British Officers called a parade and read out the 'stand fast order' to the men under their command:

In the event of an Allied invasion of Italy, Officers Commanding prison camps will ensure that prisoners of war remain within camp. Authority is granted to all Officers Commanding to take necessary disciplinary action to prevent individual prisoners of war attempting to rejoin their own units.

Many of the servicemen followed the order and as a result were seized by the Germans and sent by train to camps in Germany. In contrast, in the few prisons where the leader disobeyed the order the majority of the captives escaped.

Of the 450 New Zealanders who reached Switzerland or Allied lines, 380 or 84 per cent came from camps where all the men moved out in a group or were released by the Italians. The prisons were PG 78/1 Acquafredda, and PG 106 Vercelli, PG 107 Torviscosa, PG 120 Cetona, and their satellites. The other 70 servicemen made individual breaks from camps taken over by the Germans, from transit centres, or when being transported to Germany.

Only on 10 September did Allied HQ issue an order that the gates of all prisoner of war camps under Italian control should be opened and the prisoners advised to move towards the east coast, the south, or north in the direction of Switzerland. It was almost a week after the announcement of the Armistice before the BBC reported that the duty of escape was re-invoked.

Within four weeks of the Armistice, the British War Office circulated two secret reports on the fate of British Commonwealth prisoners of war in Italy. [2]

The first document, dated 2 October, was based on accounts of escapers who had reached Switzerland and on a report from the Vatican. The summary said that when the Armistice was signed there were about 70,000 British Commonwealth prisoners of war in Italy, located in 36 main camps and 12 military hospitals.

5

There was information on only a third of the base camps in the report. Half had been 'thrown open by the Italians' and the men freed. The other prisons had been taken over by the Germans and the inmates were being 'transferred to Germany.'

In the north-west (PM 3100), 3,500 men in total escaped from PG 133 Novara and PG 146 Mortara. At least as many were seized by the Germans at PG 5 Gavi and PG 52 Chiavari. In the rest of northern Italy (PM 3200), 2,825 prisoners were freed from three camps. PG 49 Fontanellato and PG 62 Grumello del Piano, near Bergamo, are mentioned. In contrast, a total of 5,500 men were captured from PG 19 Bologna, PG 47 Modena, PG 55 Busseto, PG 57 Grupignano and a work camp at Brescia. At least 1,950 of these POWs had already been deported. There were only two reports on prisons in central Italy (PM 3300). However, the news was positive, with escapes noted from the large camps PG 53 Sforzacosta and PG 54 Fara in Sabina. The combined number of servicemen held had been 9,771.

The prisons in the Naples area (PM 3400) and in the rest of the south (PM 3450) had been evacuated before the Armistice and the inmates sent to central and northern Italy.

The report concludes with information from the British Legation in Bern. There were nearly 1,000 Commonwealth escaped prisoners of war in Switzerland by 25 September, as well as some 'Free French' and about 1,000 Yugoslavs.

The second summary, dated 7 October, was compiled from information supplied by Allied HQ in Algiers and by the Swiss, the protecting power under the Geneva Convention. Four more camps were added to the liberated column and another to those seized by the Germans. PG 107 Torviscosa had been freed in the north-east, PG 82 Laterina, near Arezzo, in the north, and PG 78 Sulmona and PG 91 Avezzano in central Italy. In contrast, PG 21 Chieti in the same area was 'under strong Fascist guard.'

The report added that of the approximately 70,000 British Commonwealth prisoners of war in Italy at the time of the Armistice, 2,175 had reached Allied lines in the south and 1,200 had entered Switzerland. A further 26,500 servicemen were known to have been liberated and there was no information as to their recapture. Eighteen thousand prisoners of war were in German hands and 5,500 had already been transferred to Germany. There was no news as to the fate of the remaining fugitives.

The Germans used former camps and barracks as transit points for the prisoners of war they recaptured. The servicemen were sent on to the main collection centre at Mantua, known as Stalag 337, and after about 10 days entrained for Germany. The head of the Prisoner of War Division of the German High Command admitted that the transfer of prisoners was 'not carried out systematically.'

Fortunately, many of the 'other ranks' prisoners had been dispersed in a network of small work camps, which lent themselves to escape. Allied prisoners of war in Italy had been compelled to work from the summer of 1942. The employment was allowed under the Geneva Convention of 1929 if the labour provided had 'no direct relation with war operations.' Officers were excepted from the need to work and non-commissioned officers required only to undertake supervisory duties. Even before employment was made obligatory servicemen had volunteered to work on local farms and vineyards. There was the incentive of double rations, pay from a private employer and the chance to barter goods with the guards and country people.

Gradually huts were built for the detachments and the scope of the employment extended beyond agriculture. The work establishments remained satellite or sub camps of a main base. On the Armistice, the Italian guards in the small camps usually melted away or threw in their lot with the prisoners in a common desire to return home.

Events at PG 106 Vercelli in Piedmont may be taken as typical. The camp opened in the spring of 1943. At its centre was a headquarters located in a former baths building outside the railway station. The hub was administered by a major, his adjutant, a sergeant major and 30 troops.

The force coordinated 1,700 Italian soldiers involved in guarding a slightly lesser number of 'other ranks' prisoners of war located in 28 satellite camps on local farms. The servicemen were housed in stockades constructed within the courtyards of farms that had requested help in the production and harvesting of crops. The work detachments consisted of between 20 and over 100 men. On some of the holdings the prisoners lived and worked alongside female seasonal rice weeders, the *mondine*. The sub camps were commanded by lieutenants and second lieutenants brought out of retirement. They kept in touch with base by telephone, which was installed on every farm.

7

The first Allied prisoners of war arrived at Vercelli in April 1943. On 30 June there were 1,528 servicemen, made up of 455 Britons, 822 Australians, 151 New Zealanders and 100 South Africans.

The Italian Sergeant Major at PG 106 was Sergio Rigola, a 30-year-old from the nearby wool and cotton town of Biella. Over 40 years later he recalled the life of the prisoners of war at Vercelli:

As we Italians applied the Geneva Convention on Prisoners of War to the letter, every week we gave each prisoner a Red Cross parcel. They contained 26 or 28 items, including a bar of chocolate, a packet of coffee, one of sugar and another of tea, three or four tinned soups ready to heat and serve, different types of canned meat, other tins containing salmon, cheese, vegetables, condensed milk, and still more things. The prisoners also had the right to five cigarettes a day or to an equivalent quantity of tobacco with which we supplied them.

There were also cigarettes in Red Cross parcels, though I no longer remember how many. But I do know that the prisoners always had some cigarettes to give to our soldiers, or to be more precise to bribe them with, in order to obtain many small treats such as a fresh egg, or a little milk, though they were not short of the condensed variety.

One detail that left its mark on me was the abundance and variety of the groceries that arrived weekly for the prisoners in Red Cross parcels. The half kilo tins of jam were all of the *Cirio* make, Italian products that were no longer to be found here but which were probably plentiful in Britain.

However, something the prisoners were officially prohibited in any form and which they hankered after was alcohol. Our commanders continually ordered us not to give drink to the prisoners, but even though the instruction was strictly followed they managed to obtain it just the same in exchange for cigarettes or other products from the civilians with whom they came into contact.

These actions were punishable by law, but made possible and even facilitated by the fact that during wartime illegal *grappa* was distilled not far from the farmhouses of Vercelli at Cavaglià. The traffickers could have cigarettes and other valuable items for half a litre.

The civilians could even obtain goods that everyone was after, such as coffee which was no longer to be found here, and sugar which had also disappeared. And the prisoners gave willingly. They had so much that it was not a big sacrifice for them.

Sergeant Major Rigola remembered that the prisoners took perhaps three hours to carry out a job that should have taken half an hour. However, the bosses of the holdings were satisfied as long as the country tasks were completed:

The prisoners had to get up very early in the morning to go to work. Escorted by the appropriate number of guards, they were taken to the rice paddies or to the grain fields where they worked till evening.

It was difficult to control the prisoners at their place of work owing to a lack of soldiers and the fact that the men were dispersed in wide-open spaces by the needs of labour. They found themselves hundreds of metres apart and so no longer under control. The captives ably profited from these circumstances by being able to approach the civilians and indulge in their unexpected shady dealings. Given the lack of surveillance of the prisoners at work it could be said that if they had wanted to escape they could have done so, but no one ever seized the opportunity.

On the other hand, from time to time there were escape attempts by prisoners, but at night [from billets]. This took place even though the authors of earlier attempts had all been recaptured.

Several of the fugitives were even arrested close to the Swiss border after a not insubstantial time, but no one got away with it. All those who were recaptured were in possession of gold, objects of value and money, despite the weekly checks to which they were subjected. Though it was forbidden, the prisoners had all obtained these items in exchange for products which they gave the civilians.

When the captives were forced to stay behind the barbed wire all day they often indulged in sports to pass the time. They devised contests and challenges, which they carried out very noisily. If some of the men had been drinking *grappa* they made bets, even irresponsible ones such as who could get closest to the barbed wire, knowing full well that they had to maintain a distance of at least two metres. If not, they would be ordered to halt by a sentry and threatened with being shot. This was what happened to one of the prisoners who disobeyed the rule. He was killed by a soldier following the regulations more strictly than was normal.

On other occasions, the prisoners would try to confuse the detachment commanders at the evening roll call. English names presented problems to us Italians. One of the men would reply in place of another who might be absent. After a while the process became so confused that the commandant had to suspend it.

These are all things that either I experienced or were reported to me by one or other of four prisoners who spoke Italian and had been transferred to our headquarters at Vercelli as interpreters. They helped us in the distribution of the numerous parcels that the prisoners received from home. The quartet became indispensable for these operations as they practically knew by heart the detachments in which their fellow soldiers could be found and in half a minute could read 30 names. The men carried out these tasks diligently, saving us Italians from the difficult task of dealing with names which were not only unpronounceable but also very similar.

With troubles of this nature, with problems of more or less importance that had to be dealt with on a daily basis, the spring passed and also most of the summer.

Then 8 September arrived and the proclamation over the radio at 8pm by Marshal Badoglio of the news of the signing of the Armistice between us and the Anglo-Americans.

This dramatic event caused confusion and bewilderment at the PG 106 Headquarters. The first effects were already apparent on the morning of 9 September. The Adjutant, a captain from Turin, made himself scarce. He said that he was going home to obtain orders, though we had heard on the telephone that the Germans had already occupied the High Command in the city.

At around midday it was the turn of the Commandant, a major, who presented himself at the headquarters of the Vercelli garrison even though he knew the Germans were already there. The 30 soldiers that were with me also profited from the confusion and stole away.

I was the only person still at his post. I was preoccupied by what had happened, by the telephone calls and by the reports and rumours that said the Germans were occupying the city and the military and logistical centres of our country. I was troubled by anxious questions that arrived over the phone from the various detachments. They asked for news of the situation and what they should do.

As a precaution and to avoid being taken by surprise I changed into civilian clothing. No one bothered me, but from my window I was met with the terrible sight of hundreds of uniformed Italian soldiers formed into columns and guarded by German troops being taken to the station at Vercelli for transportation to who knows where.

It was really that image and my memory of Badoglio's statement that the prisoners of war should be defended that led me to take the action that I do not regret to this day. I picked up the telephone and spoke to the commandants of the detachments. I ordered that all the prisoners should be freed. For the officers it was sufficient to hear a voice from headquarters. They knew full well that it was not the Commandant speaking but Sergeant Major Rigola. But they responded immediately to the order, carried it out and cut all the strings.

I stayed to continue my work for the whole of 9 September. I acted as God Almighty and had all the prisoners freed. Once I had finished, I threw the keys under the door and went home. [3]

Once the 'stand fast order' unravelled, escaped Allied prisoners of war were dependent upon Italian civilians and members of the Resistance for food, shelter and protection. Each encounter created a distinctive story, many of which are still remembered.

Shortly after the Armistice, factory worker Giordano Baini was at the railway station in Colico on the north-eastern tip of Lake Como. The 24-year-old worked across the lake at an electronics factory in Gravedona and returned to his home in Milan each weekend.

On this occasion, Giordano noticed that two men in civilian clothing were staring nervously at Fascist militia overseeing the ticket hall. He heard the strangers talking quietly in a language that was neither Italian nor German. The worker guessed that the men were escaped British prisoners of war. In broken Italian they

11

told him they were making for the Swiss border but had almost run out of money. Giordano quickly bought the fugitives tickets for Chiavenna, 27 kilometres along the line, the last station before the frontier and the Alpine passes. As the local train steamed into the station the two escapers surged forward with the rest of the crowd. [4]

Two gunnery officers who had escaped from PG 49 Fontanellato were sheltered by the farming community to the west of Pellegrino Parmense. Captain John W Fairbrass from Colchester and Lieutenant FG Cook from north London stayed with Guerino and Maria Vernazza at Ceriato. Their daughter, Irma, recalled:

> The prisoners lived with us for part of the week and then spent some time with my aunt, Zelinda Giordani, who lived in the valley opposite at Casa Veronica. When the officers wanted to come back to us we devised a signal. If all was well, we would leave the kitchen curtains open so that they could see the light and know that it was safe to return.

Captain Fairbrass was among the escapers my grandparents, Alfredo and Giuseppina Dall' Arda, and my mother, Clara, also helped from Castell' Arquato. The two officers were still in the area in April 1944, but were subsequently recaptured and sent to German camps. I was able to pass on this information to Irma, who said: 'We always wondered what became of them.' [5]

* * *

Winston Churchill wrote that one of the greatest achievements of the insurgent movement was 'the succour and support given to our prisoners of war trapped by the Armistice in camps in northern Italy.' He added:

> Out of about eighty thousand of these men, conspicuously clothed in battle dress, and in the main with little knowledge of the language or geography of the country, at least ten thousand, mostly helped by the local population with civilian clothes, were guided to safety, thanks to the risks taken by members of the Italian Resistance and the simple people of the countryside. [6]

12

In the months prior to September 1943, Churchill had stressed the importance of the immediate liberation of all British prisoners of war and the prevention of their being transported northwards to Germany. After the Armistice and the German occupation and Fascist revival the only possibility was damage limitation. The official rescue work is the theme of the next chapter.

NOTES

[1] Winston S Churchill, *The Second World War, Volume V, Closing the Ring*, pp 99-100.
[2] The National Archives of the UK (TNA): Public Record Office (PRO) - hereafter TNA: PRO - WO 224/179. In books, documents and everyday speech 'British' was often used as shorthand for subjects of the British Crown throughout the Empire and Commonwealth.
[3] Luigi Moranino, 'Il campo di prigionia PG 106,' *l' impegno*, April 1989, Istituto per la storia della Resistenza e della società contemporanea nelle province di Biella e Vercelli. The translations of this and other Italian sources are mine.
[4] Information credit: Fiorenzo Baini, Milan.
[5] Information credit: Irma Vernazza, London. Thanks also to Mayor Roberto Ventura of Pellegrino Parmense for providing the names of families in the commune who helped escapers. See my book, *British Prisoners of War in Italy: Paths to Freedom* for the mass escape from PG 49 Fontanellato and the story of the servicemen who remained in the area, some for 15 months.
[6] Churchill, op. cit., pp 166-7.

Camp money from PG 73 Carpi, near Modena, kindly
supplied by Oscar D'Alcorn, one of the former prisoners.
On the Armistice of September 1943, the Germans took
over and the inmates were sent to a camp in Austria.

2 ESCAPE AND EVASION

The British organisation with the unenviable task of rescuing thousands of prisoners of war in Italy after the September 1943 Armistice was the secret service codenamed MI 9. Its global mission, as set out by the wartime commander, Brigadier Norman Crockatt, DSO, MC, was:

(a) To facilitate escapes of British prisoners of war, thereby getting back service personnel and containing additional enemy manpower on guard duties.
(b) To facilitate the return to the United Kingdom of those who succeeded in evading capture in enemy-occupied territory.
(c) To collect and distribute information.
(d) To assist in the denial of information to the enemy.
(e) To maintain morale of British prisoners of war in enemy prison camps.

MI 9 initially operated in the Mediterranean as N Section. It was under the overall direction of A Force, the deception and escape organisation attached to Allied Force Headquarters Mediterranean (AFHQ). From August 1944, MI 9 used the cover name of IS 9 (CMF). IS 9 originally referred to MI 9's Intelligence School set up in Highgate, north London.

Field sections in Italy were inter-Allied as well as inter-service. The United States had created its own escape and evasion agency in October 1942. It was codenamed MIS-X and commanded by Lieutenant Colonel J Edward Johnston. In this chapter we concentrate on two key operational areas for Allied search and rescue in the early days, the south-east coast and the border with Yugoslavia.

The head of N Section, Lieutenant Colonel Anthony Simonds, landed with the invading 1st British Airborne Division of the Eighth Army at Taranto. He had been urgently summoned to AFHQ Algiers from Cairo and ordered to do everything possible to rescue Allied prisoners of war in Italy on the express instructions of Winston Churchill. Simonds was a regular soldier with expertise in intelligence and experience of irregular warfare as an SOE agent. He set up his headquarters at Bari, chief town of the Puglia region.

As a first measure, field escape sections were organised. They went as far as 60 miles inside enemy-held territory, locating

15

escapers and evaders, providing them with money, compasses and maps, and directing them through the lines. Detachments operated with the Fifth Army in the western sector of the front and with the Eighth Army in the centre and at Termoli in the east. The port became a forward base and home to the section's private navy. It was mainly crewed by Italians and included an infantry landing craft (LCI) that could easily carry 250 men.

The commander of the No. 2 Field Escape Section attached to Eighth Army was Captain Christopher Soames, later Churchill's son-in-law and the Conservative politician. His orders were 'to utilise all known available means to produce a network of helpers behind the enemy lines and make local plans for the early rescue of ground troops and air crews at large within enemy territory.'

In October, a large-scale operation was launched to rescue former prisoners of war along the Adriatic. A variety of regular and special forces were deployed in a multinational unit known as Simcol. It worked along the open and less densely populated stretch of coastline running from Ancona in the Marches down to Pescara in the Abruzzo.

The commander of one of the elements involved in the rescue effort, Lieutenant Colonel William Stirling of 2 SAS, did not see the role as appropriate for his men. Squadron leader, Major Roy Farran, reflected general opinion in the service when he wrote five years later:

The first operation had only an indirect connection with the war. Many British prisoners had escaped at the time of the surrender and were now at large behind the enemy lines. In response to pressure brought to bear by politicians at home, a force was organised to do what it could to facilitate their rescue. We were the tools. A number of small parties equipped with wireless sets were dropped in the foothills all along the Adriatic coast from Ancona to Pescara. Their job was to direct ex prisoners to beach parties who had been landed from motor torpedo boats on the coast. Between the beach parties and the parachutists in the hills, foot parties of SAS would act as guides. Periodically landing craft or motor torpedo boats would come into the beach parties in answer to a torch signal to pick up the refugees.

The operation went on for two months but was never an outstanding success. There were many reasons. Sometimes large parties of ex prisoners got down to the beaches alright, but they were usually scattered by the Germans before they could be picked up. The Navy found it difficult to make exact landfalls on a featureless beach, and above all most of the prisoners were so demoralised that they were not prepared to exert themselves. Contrary to popular opinion at home, many of them preferred to stay in comparative safety in an Italian farm than to risk their necks in a hazardous escape. [1]

On 7 November, Captain Soames reported to Wing Commander EH Dennis, in charge of the MI 9 base with Major JV Fillingham, that his constant problem was to keep parties of escapers on the move. They had an annoying inclination to loiter whenever they found a beautiful valley or a pretty girl. In addition, most of the men showed a complete lack of gratitude to their guides and took them completely for granted.

Four beach parties from 2 SAS were landed at strategic points along the coast in Operation Jonquil. The French SAS Squadron provided a covering party.

Between 2 and 6 October, four detachments of the Eighth Army's 1st Airborne and another from 2 SAS were parachuted to various points inland in the complementary Operation Begonia. The force successfully located hundreds of prisoners and shepherded them to boat rendezvous, but owing to radio problems and disruption caused by a German counter-attack on the new Allied base at Termoli only 50 men were eventually rescued.

The American component in the relief force was a detachment from the Italian Operational Group (Company A) of the Office of Strategic Services (OSS). The section of 15 uniformed Italian Americans from Station X in Algiers was led by Lieutenant Peter Sauro. Ten of the soldiers were parachuted into the south of the zone on 2 October. They split into three groups to cover a wider area. The remaining five men were assigned to the British SAS as interpreters and went in by sea.

Lieutenant Sauro and three enlisted men were captured by the enemy in January 1944 and spent the rest of the war in German camps. Other members of the task force remained behind enemy lines until March. [2]

Lieutenant Colonel Simonds reported that 822 Allied escapers and evaders were rescued by A Force up to the end of November

17

1943. Almost a thousand more servicemen crossed the lines without official help. Liberated servicemen were speedily sent to transit camps at Bari, Naples and Taranto, where they were debriefed prior to repatriation.

By 1944, Fascist spies and German reprisals led the civilian population to distrust outsiders. A British agent had also come close to being shot by escaped prisoners. It became more productive to use Italian operatives behind the lines and Allied special forces to provide covering parties for the sea evacuations. The agents were usually drawn from elite units of the disbanded Italian Armed Forces such as military intelligence, the artillery and parachutists.

Two star operatives were Naval lieutenant the Marquis Ugo Ranieri di Bourbon, with the alias of Hugh, and Captain Andrew Losco, known as John. The lieutenant ran escape lines to the Adriatic coast which saved more than 400 men. The captain broke out of Macerata gaol in May 1944 and speedily moved to the Tenna Valley, fifteen miles to the south-east. He teamed up with a dynamic British agent, Captain Jock McKee. In September the Italian was in action near Maribor in Slovenia, helping evacuate 100 Allied servicemen by air before again being arrested. He was eventually freed by the Allies during the final offensive. [3]

Five days before Christmas 1943, a party of eleven escapers arrived by fishing boat at Termoli from Cattolica. They were the most senior Allied former prisoners of war in Italy, generals Philip Neame and Richard O' Connor and Air Vice Marshal Boyd, together with a South African private, two British officer agents and five Italian helpers. Five months later, five brigadiers and eleven other escapers also arrived by boat. They had been rescued by Captain Losco and other top N Section agents and taken off from near Fermo. A few days later reports came in that the Germans were disguising agents as escapers to entrap helpers, while at the same time offering a reward of 5,000 lire to informers. Five or six renegade Allied ex POWs were aiding the enemy.

On 24 May 1944, two Allied rescue craft left Termoli in Operation Darlington II. The vessels became separated during the journey north. American patrol boat P-402 made the rendezvous at the mouth of the River Tenna and exchanged signals with shore. At a distance of a hundred yards a sailor was sent towards the beach with two dinghies, but mysteriously disappeared, though the sea was calm and he wore a lifebelt. The captain, Lieutenant Gene Moritz, was forced to beach his 63-foot craft. Twenty-six escapers and evaders were embarked and the boat kedged off.

The second craft, the British LCI, also eventually reached the estuary, but found no servicemen and turned for home. Several miles southward the correct light sequence was seen coming from an unknown secluded beach. A commando covering party was sent ashore. It discovered 127 escapers and evaders. They were embarked within half an hour. Major Fillingham claimed the operation as undoubtedly the most successful pickup conducted by any service anywhere in Italy.

Captain Peter Fowler was A Force's key organiser on the western coast. He was entrusted with infiltrating agents into the north under the overall direction of headquarters in Algiers. Sea operations were mounted using No. 1 Special Force's private navy run out of Bastia in Corsica by Captain Andrew Croft. A total of six agents were landed in two operations conducted in February and April 1944, but three other attempts were unsuccessful owing to lack of reception committees. Fourteen escapers were also plucked from the beaches on 19 February. They reached Corsica two days later in a small boat.

* * *

One of the evaders in south-eastern Italy was Peter Coxell, a sergeant with 250 Squadron RAF. He piloted a Curtiss P-40 Kittyhawk, a single-engine, single-seater fighter-bomber, from Mileni, one of the Foggia group of airbases. This is his story:

At 0600 hours on 3 November 1943 four of us were sitting in our cockpits, waiting for first light to take off on an armed reconnaissance. We were supplied with a mug of tea by the mess corporal. We flew up the coast to slightly above Ancona and turned inland to look for targets. Passing over Jesi airdrome we saw two Italian aircraft and the leader decided to strafe them as there was nothing else on offer.

After attacking and pulling up I saw the red light on the dash flashing to indicate engine overheating. Glycol was also pouring out of my exhaust stubs. The altimeter showed 1,500 feet above sea level, but not knowing the height of the terrain I decided to force land rather than bale out. Had I jumped I would have been tracked by the enemy and captured. Instead, I travelled some distance away from the coastal area occupied by the Germans.

I opened the cockpit hood, locked it back and tightened my safety harness. It was a wheels-up landing. I slid to rather an abrupt halt in a reasonably level field, which was covered with low grapevines. At once I was approached by some of the locals. They seemed surprised that I was on my own. The long-range tank had been brushed off at first contact and left many yards behind. The Italians thought it was a bomb until we managed to find the word *benzina*, petrol, and all was well. I was ushered into the nearest isolated farmhouse and put in a loft. I stayed for 36 hours. I was kited out with civilian clothing and had visits from several residents. Among them was Doctor Tommaso Giretti, starting a wonderful relationship with the family. On the second day he arrived in his little Fiat 500. I was folded into the rear seat with my head down and driven to his house at Cerividone, five or six miles away. The nearest town was Cignola, in the centre of the Le Marche region.

I was introduced to Ralph and John, two South Africans who had escaped from their POW camp near Padua at the time of the Armistice. Ralph's surname was Selby. He was a bombardier in the South African artillery and had been taken prisoner at Tobruk. I never knew John's surname because our relationship was very brief. He absconded into the night a couple of days later. He was quite short and dark, whereas Ralph and I were both six-foot and fair-haired. John obviously thought he stood a better chance on his own. We never heard of him again.

Peter and Ralph decided to walk south in the hope of crossing the lines, a distance of 150 miles as the crow flies. On 20 November, they met a British officer near Civitanuova. He introduced himself as Captain Simpson and told them of a plan for a night-time evacuation by landing craft. Peter Coxell recalled:

We were given a map reference and told to meet on the 22nd. I wondered if the officer gave his correct name for security reasons. After negotiating the busy coastal road and railway used by the enemy we made our rendezvous on the beach. Though it was pitch dark I estimated there were

20 or 30 people there. Many were smoking in spite of being told not to do so. After some hours, and assuming signals had been made seaward, we were told the rescue was not going ahead. We were instructed to repeat the exercise two days later, but this met with the same lack of success. We lost touch with the operation and by 1 December were again heading south ...

We followed a regular routine. During the day we kept clear of any villages and either approached a solitary worker in the fields or called on an isolated farmhouse and asked for a glass of water, openly explaining that we were escaped British prisoners of war. The result was invariably great sympathy, something basic to eat and a glass of *vino*. Often we would be given a hunk of homebaked bread drizzled with olive oil and a touch of salt.

The evening routine would be to select a very secluded farmhouse and wait until dusk before approaching. The reception would be the same. Pasta in its many forms was the basic diet, together with polenta, bean soup and the nice crusty bread that every house made two or three times a week. Very little meat was seen. A few slices of homemade salami were regarded as a treat.

On 8 January 1944, the two friends joined a group of Italians who were hoping to cross the lines with the help of a local guide. However, after four days the attempt was abandoned near Chieti as too dangerous. The servicemen decided to return to Cerividone. Ralph had contacted jaundice and would benefit from the care of Doctor Giretti. After slow progress in bad weather the pair reached the village on 2 March. Ralph was immediately put to bed at the doctor's and Peter was sent to stay with a farmer called Guido and his wife in their isolated farmhouse a few miles away.

At the end of March, Doctor Giretti told Peter that the partisans were organising an escape and had been instructed to give priority to aircrew. The sergeant joined other evaders under a tarpaulin in the back of a low-sided lorry. The driver was a giant of a man with red hair. He turned out to be an escaped British POW who had joined the Resistance. Two partisans armed with Sten guns accompanied the men. As evening approached the vehicle suddenly slowed down and then accelerated violently to the accompaniment of shouts and machine gun fire. It was a

Fascist roadblock. After about 20 minutes flight the driver said that he was going to destroy the lorry. The men scattered, relieved to have escaped without injury. Peter made his way back to Cerividone. He recalled subsequent events:

I was back at the small farm with Guido for a while, but on 4 April the balloon went up. We were told to flee as Tommaso and another man had been arrested by the Fascists. We immediately started south once more and kept gently on the move throughout April and May, making some reliable contacts. The weather was better, making life much easier. We were spending nights out in the open as a safety measure and there was plenty of cover in the cornfields.

We were also encouraged by the endless rumours of the advances being made by the Allies to the south. We were hearing gunfire from this direction. We were told that the Germans were pulling back, looting cattle and supplies.

The actual crossing of the front was an anticlimax. The noise seemed to get closer and then there was a complete lull for perhaps a day. We suddenly realised the battle noises were now behind us, to the north. We decided to travel east towards the coastal area where the advance would obviously be taking place. Around 15 June we sighted a Sherman tank and were able to make contact with the Allies in the form of the Polish Brigade.

Peter Coxell had been promoted to Flight Sergeant in his absence and later became a Flying Officer. After returning to the United Kingdom, he flew Spitfires with 127 Squadron RAF in the Second Tactical Airforce for the rest of the war. [4]

* * *

For many escapers and evaders in the plains surrounding the Gulf of Venice the main hope of freedom lay in following the difficult route through Slovenia, then Italy's most north-easterly region, across a divided Yugoslavia, and over the Adriatic by air or sea to liberated southern Italy.

During most of the journey guides and protection had to be sought from insurgents, mainly Communists and royalist Chetniks. These were not the new bands of Italy, but in Churchill's words, 'hardy and hunted guerrillas,' who had been fighting the Germans since 1941 and had already withstood five enemy offensives.

After the Armistice of September 1943, six Italian divisions in Yugoslavia were disarmed. Two others threw in their lot with the partisans and formed the Garibaldi and Matteotti battalions. With Italian equipment the irregulars had been able to field 80,000 more men and to occupy most of the coastline.

A network of Allied missions was soon attached to the main rebel formations. These included 11 in territory running from Slovenia to the Bulgarian border dominated by the Communist leader Josip Broz, better known as Tito. However, relations with the Yugoslavs were characterised by constant arguments and mutual incomprehension.

On 11 October 1943, two British officer escapers, Ballentine and Gibbon, arrived at a special camp set up by the partisans at Caporetto in the Julian Alps from which mixed platoons of Commonwealth escapers were already launching raids on German patrols. The officers rapidly came to the conclusion that the men should be extricated. Major EH Gibbon, DSO and Bar, of the Royal Tank Regiment, reported to the War Office that the partisans lived by raiding local villages. Cooperation with them was almost impossible owing to differences in language and training. Half of the servicemen were poorly dressed in civilian clothing. All said that they had only taken up arms because they felt under obligation to the partisans for helping them and that they intended to leave as soon as the opportunity arose.

The partisan headquarters reacted angrily to the proposed defection of their Allied detachment, but finally gave permission for a party of 85 men to leave on 17 October. Four other servicemen chose to remain with the rebels.

The slow journey south involved long marches over difficult terrain and in poor weather conditions. The Germans were often on the group's heels and the partisans obstructive. Captain DJ Riddiford, a New Zealander from 6 Field Regiment, acted as interpreter. He recalled:

> We were passed from command to command, sometimes spending a few hours with different units of Tito's variegated forces, sometimes days, and on one occasion over a week. Always there were interminable discussions with the partisans, always the same difficulties in persuading them to agree to our plans. Once we were held

captive for over a week, four days being spent in the open with rain falling and snow threatening. With the first winter snow on the ground they flatly refused to give us any guides or escort on account of a large scale German roundup of partisans. Major Gibbon led the party with a home-made compass belonging to me across 30 miles of country dominated by the Germans into which no partisan would venture.

The captain was awarded the Military Cross for his actions. The escapers entered Yugoslav territory north of Idria. Forty of the men with poorer footwear and clothing were detached and followed on at a slower pace, but were scattered by enemy fire. Twenty-two subsequently rejoined the main party and one or two others made contact with later groups of escapers.

The fugitives were finally taken 140 miles by truck to the partisan headquarters at Otocac. The men were treated to a sumptuous feast in recognition of British and American airdrops to the Resistance. After a stay of 18 days the party was picked up by fishing boat from Senj on the Dalmatian Coast and conducted to a rendezvous with a landing craft on the island of Vis. The vessel hove to in Bari harbour on 23 December with 62 escapers on board. Shortly afterwards, the sixth German offensive cleared the partisans from the key points on the coastline and from all but two of the islands.

A more fruitful airborne phase of the rescue work opened in the spring of 1944. The Allies had decided to withdraw support from the royalist General Mihailović and to recall the missions operating in his territory. Aid was only to be channelled to Marshal Tito and his National Committee of Liberation. This policy was based on the conviction, in the British Ambassador's words on Christmas Day 1943, that the Communists would be 'the rulers of Yugoslavia.' He added: 'They are of such value to us militarily that we must back them to the full, subordinating political considerations to military.' The marshal authorised the reception of new Allied missions. These included liaison teams from A Force and MIS-X.

Escape lines were created and a transit camp was opened at Crnomelj. A landing strip was built nearby, as well as another at Glina. British Liaison Officers east of Verona were instructed to direct escapers and evaders through Yugoslavia. In September, additional A Force agents were sent to Slovenia and north-east of

Ljubljana. As well as men from Italy, the fugitives included prisoners who had escaped from camps in Austria and aircrew shot down over the Balkans.

Personnel drops and evacuations in the Balkans and Italy were the responsibility of the multinational squadrons under the control of the Royal Air Force's No. 334 Wing, based at Brindisi in south-eastern Italy. The main aircraft used was the C-47 Douglas Dakota transporter (the DC-3), which was particularly suited to the rough airfields improvised in the interior.

From February to the end of March 1944, and again from October, special duties operations were carried out by the United States Army Air Force (USAAF) Dakota squadrons of the 62nd Troop Carrier Group (TCG), which alternated with the 60th TCG.

The Royal Air Force also sent four of its Dakotas from No. 267 Squadron at Bari. Apart from the period 1 April to 5 May, when it was deployed on the Italy-Cairo run, the squadron engaged in special duties for the rest of the year. No. 44 Squadron South African Air Force (SAAF) replaced the unit in January 1945.

There was even a Soviet flight. In March 1944, one of two Dakotas used to fly a Russian mission to Italy was designated for supply drops to Yugoslav partisans and placed under the operational control of No. 267 Squadron. On 25 August, the force was expanded to 12 Dakotas, as well as 12 Yak-9 fighters, with a complement of 80 ground and air crew under a full colonel. The unit made airdrops to the Russian mission in Yugoslavia and also took part in 334 Wing's general operations, though a later American report said that RAF control was 'more nominal than real, the Russians throughout taking an extremely independent line.' [5] In October 1944, the Soviet group evacuated 855 personnel from the Balkans, including 114 Allied aircrew.

Other squadrons from 334 Wing concentrated on supply drops to the partisans and to Allied missions and parties of escapers. The Royal Air Force provided the Polish Flight 1586 and No. 148 Squadron, which also had small Lysander flight for landings. Two squadrons of the Co-Belligerent Italian Air Force, based at Lecce, joined the wing in February 1944. The 1st Squadron was equipped with Cant Z 1007s and the 88th Squadron with Savoia Marchetti SM 82 heavy bomber/transports.

In October 1944, the USAAF 885th Bombardment Squadron also began special duty flights from Brindisi. In December, it was reinforced by the 859th Squadron, nicknamed 'the Spooks,' which was detached from 492nd Bombardment Group, based at

Harrington in Northamptonshire. The 885th Squadron primarily deployed its Liberators and Flying Fortresses on Italian missions, and the 859th Squadron, which only flew Liberators, concentrated on Yugoslavia, but both formations operated in the same area if required by weather conditions. On 20 January 1945, the squadrons formed the 15th Special Group (Provisional), which was redesignated the 2641st Special Group (Provisional) on 6 March. Three weeks later the unit moved north to Rosignano. By this time the airfield was also home to the Dakotas of 64th TCG, which together with the 62nd Group at Tarquinia carried out most supply and personnel dropping over northern Italy. Another Tuscan airport at Malignano was also sometimes used. From February 1945 it replaced Brindisi as the main SOE despatch centre.

In addition to the dedicated squadrons, aircraft and crews were seconded from 205 Bomber Group. Number 178 Squadron RAF and 31 and 34 SAAF squadrons assisted 148 Squadron and the Polish Flight in ferrying supplies to support the Warsaw rising in August and September 1944. From late October 1944, the group's entire force of 54 Liberators and 80 Wellingtons was deployed in supply dropping as well as in bombing raids, across Italy, the Balkans and south-eastern Europe.

In Yugoslavia, tactical squads were parachuted in to build and manage covert airstrips in a programme named the Balkans Air Terminal Service. The partisans provided handling parties. Thirty-six landing grounds were eventually created across the country.

The Dakotas of 334 Wing were used in Operation Repartee to evacuate Allied personnel from General Mihailović's headquarters in central Yugoslavia. On 28 May 1944, an aircraft flown by Wing Commander AN Francombe of 267 Squadron landed safely on a short runway and left with 20 passengers. A second plane followed the next night, captained by Flight Lieutenant JD Rice. This time only 15 men were evacuated owing to safety concerns. At the last minute the Chetniks refused to allow the head of the mission, Brigadier Armstrong, DSO, MC, and seven other officers to depart. The crisis was diffused by the arrival of American Dakotas from 60th TCG on the 30th with senior partisan leaders onboard and a message from the Commander-in-Chief. In total, 120 Allied personnel were rescued, including the British and American missions, escaped prisoners of war and downed aircrew.

The Americans retained a single intelligence mission with the general on the express orders of President Roosevelt and it continued to support rescue work. Mihailović allowed landing strips to remain in such territory as he controlled and his commanders to provide guides and protection for escapers and evaders. In 1946, the general was captured and executed by the Communists after a show trial.

Two years later, President Truman posthumously awarded the soldier the highest possible award for a foreign national, the Legion of Merit, on the recommendation of General Dwight D Eisenhower. The citation recognised the rescue of over 500 United States airmen among approximately 600 helped by Chetnik forces. News of the award and the circumstances were classified by the State Department and not publicised for over a decade.

On 15 June 1944, the Balkan Air Force (BAF) was created at Bari. This inter-Allied headquarters coordinated air, land, sea and special operations in the Adriatic area and the Aegean and Ionian Seas. The commander was RAF Vice Marshal William Elliot. The air component mounted fighter attacks on enemy forces and communications, carried out the largest air supply of partisans in the European campaign and evacuated thousands of escapers and evaders and wounded partisans. Number 334 Wing was attached to the new force. A directive issued in January 1945 stated that the Balkans was to be the wing's main priority, with targets and tasks set by BAF. The secondary mission to Italy would follow the directions of the Mediterranean Allied Air Force, based at Caserta.

Late in 1944 German troops in Yugoslavia began to withdraw north, allowing sea evacuations of escapers and evaders to recommence. The route from Italy ran through Cividale del Friuli and Gorizia, into Slovenia and on to Postumia, east to Novo Mesto and Metlika, and then south of Zagreb in Croatia to Glina. From there a truck service ferried the men across the mountains to the coast and a rendezvous with an Allied craft.

A large group of escapers left Zara in a British battleship on the last day of 1944. The men had been assembled from different parties sent by military missions in north-eastern Italy. The final escape was organised in December by a New Zealander, Lance Corporal D Russell. The party arrived in Bari on 11 February 1945, but the escape agent was captured by the Germans and executed. He was posthumously awarded the George Cross.

At the end of December 1944 the Germans launched a massive offensive against the partisans in northern Slovenia to clear the way for the passage of their army in retreat from the south. Allied agents were withdrawn from the area and the escape line officially came to an end. Over two thousand Allied aircrew and several hundred former prisoners of war had regained their freedom by using the route.

*   *   *

In November 1944, it was estimated that at least 2,156 servicemen had been rescued by MI 9 in Italy since the Armistice. At a meeting held at the Bari headquarters between its co-commandant, Wing Commander Dennis, and four Resistance leaders from the north, Ferruccio Parri of the Action Party said there were 'some hundreds' of escapers living with families in the Po Valley. He agreed to instruct all partisan groups to give every help to IS 9. The Wing Commander defined the priorities for rescuing escapers and evaders. First came special forces, then downed aircrew, next those involved in the current campaign and finally prisoners of war from earlier conflicts.

The list reveals the main source of new escapers and evaders in the last winter of the war. It also underlines the reality that successful rescue work depended to a large extent on Italians. The escape lines created and run by the Resistance are the topic of the next chapter.

NOTES

[1] Roy Farran, *Winged Dagger*, pp 199-200.
[2] Information credit: Albert Materazzi, United States, Operations Officer, OSS Italian Operational Group. An Army Captain, he operated in Algeria, Corsica, Siena and Florence, and was awarded the USA Legion of Merit.
[3] All partisans and Allied agents adopted a pseudonym or *nome di battaglia*. These are shown in brackets after proper names or in inverted commas on their own.
[4] Information credit: The narrative is based on a manuscript kindly supplied by Peter Coxell, Henley-on-Thames.
[5] Air Historical Office, HQ Army Air Forces, *Special Operations: AAF Aid to European Resistance Movements 1943-1945*, Washington: 1947.

3 THE 'UNDERGROUND RAILWAY'

The main rescue organisation for Allied servicemen in northern Italy was a branch of the Italian Resistance known as the *Ufficio Assistenza Prigionieri di Guerra Alleati*, or the Service for Assisting Allied Prisoners of War. It was more commonly known as the Milan Network.

The agency was created as early as 20 September 1943 on the orders of Ferruccio Parri, leader of the Action Party and commandant of its *Giustizia e Libertà* partisan formations. Like the Allies, he believed that the rescue work was a vital part of the war effort. In addition, the Resistance had to fulfil the Armistice obligations of the former Rome government.

Organising the escape line was entrusted to engineer Giuseppe Bacciagaluppi, Managing Director of the Italian subsidiary of the American Standard Electric Corporation, which manufactured telecommunications equipment. He was married to an Englishwoman called Audrey Smith. As well as a residence in Milan the couple had a holiday home at Caldè on Lake Maggiore.

The *Centro Cardinal Ferrari*, Fontanellato, Parma, formerly camp number 49.

The service not only operated across Lombardy, but also in the neighbouring regions of Piedmont, Emilia and the Veneto. The main activity was undertaken by the Milan Committee of National Liberation. It was supported by subsidiary Resistance organisations and by private groups or individuals able to give direct help or donate money. Vast funds were required to sustain the servicemen in their hiding places and to conduct them to the border. This usually involved rail travel and sometimes also the purchase of bicycles and rowing boats. During the final dangerous border crossing, payments were needed for what official reports described as 'professional guides,' who were in reality *contrabbandieri*, or smugglers. They usually charged 100 lire a time.

When the venture went smoothly it took only a day or two to transport the servicemen to the sanctuary of Switzerland. The help was especially valuable during the winter months. By December 1943 the high mountain routes were almost impassable and protected by strong garrisons. In Macugnaga at the foot of Monte Rosa, for example, there was a force of 300 Germans.

Two groups of escapers made contact with the organisation in the Padua area at this time. They were all New Zealanders, four from work camp PG 120/5 at Abano and five from PG 107 Torviscosa in the plains north-east of Venice. Within days all the men had been taken by train to Como, across the lake by boat and over the mountains to Switzerland.

One of the engineer's lieutenants was another English-speaking Milanese industrialist, an iron and steel manufacturer called Ulisse Cantoni. Aged 40, he was tall and slim, wore well-tailored suits and rode a motorcycle. From September 1943 to April 1944 Cantoni acted as District Agent for the Assistance Service in two of Lombardy's nine provinces, Milan itself and Pavia. Bacciagaluppi recalled:

> Ulisse Cantoni was one of our most active and selfless helpers. He organised transport and journeys, as well as contributing substantial amounts of money, food and clothing for the prisoners, both directly and through our organisation. With great enthusiasm and disregard for his own safety, Ulisse personally guided the more than 100 prisoners of war who were entrusted to his care to the Swiss frontier.

Cantoni's clandestine activities began on 25 September 1943. At first working alone, he rescued 42 prisoners from an 'other ranks' camp at Vairano, north-east of Pavia. The men were split into five groups and taken to Moltasio on the western shore of Lake Como. From there it was only a short journey to the Swiss border near Chiasso. The Italians favoured this direct route. It ran through a populous area, but offered the easiest passage. Cantoni soon found an able assistant in a worker from Lodi called Pietro Bacchi. Sadly, he was executed by the Germans together with three other partisans in August 1944.

Most of the prisoners were from work camps located in the countryside to the west of Milan. The men usually stayed at Cantoni's house at 50, Via Vallazze, Milan, for about two days before leaving for Switzerland, though on one occasion six remained for ten days. The Italian and four servicemen were once arrested by the Fascist police, but they attacked their guards and escaped.

Ulisse Cantoni helped at least 133 prisoners of war, 90 British, 37 South Africans, 5 Yugoslavs and a single Pole. He related that this was the number of slips left by escapers, or at least, those he was able to find after the war.

Ulisse Cantoni, District Organiser, Milan Network. (Bryson)

Norman and Richard Haw, Egypt, October 1941. (Bryson)

South African escapers in Arosa, Switzerland: (left to right) Sam van Wyk, Richard Haw, Costin and Happle. (Bryson)

Typical of the men the businessman assisted was the unusual pairing of Corporal Richard Haw, a veteran of the First World War, and his eldest son, Norman, a private. Both were volunteers in the South African Umvoti Mounted Rifles, which marched into captivity on the fall of Tobruk in June 1942. The Second Division of 10,722 men was moved to Italy by sea before the end of the year. Richard and Norman recalled that the prisoners were pelted with rotten tomatoes when they landed at Naples.

After being held in the transit camp PG 66 Capua and at PG 54 Fara in Sabina, the men were transferred to a satellite camp of PG 146 Mortara in April 1943. A secret British report on the camps in Italy noted that the base controlled 2,344 'other ranks' prisoners at the end of June 1943, made up of 610 South Africans and 1,734 Britons. They were accommodated in 'large farmhouses.' Work camp three was at Ferrera Erbognone on the left bank of the River Po, 27 kilometres west of Pavia, in the Lomellina, the great rice growing area to the west of Milan. Camp 146 was the largest of three in the north-west thrown open by the Italians on the Armistice so that 4,689 prisoners were liberated. The other camps were close by: PG 106 Vercelli, which we have already visited, and PG 133 Novara. In contrast, 3,916 men held at PG 5 Gavi in Piedmont and at PG 52 Chiavari in Liguria rapidly fell into German hands.

The two South Africans were released on 10 September. In their escape reports they recalled: 'We went back to the farm where we had worked. We stayed around about here for three months, being clothed and fed by the farmers who finally arranged our journey to Switzerland.' [1] The main helper was Luigi Moro of Sannazzaro.

The escape attempt was made at the beginning of December. Richard and Norman were met by a guide in Ferrera Erbognone and taken by train to Milan. At some stage the soldiers encountered the district organiser, Ulisse Cantoni. In the evening the riflemen were taken the short 75-kilometre train journey to Bellano on Lake Como. They crossed by boat to the western shore and trekked to a hut on the mountainside. Two days later, on 5 December, guides led the escapers over rough trails to Carena in Switzerland. They were sent to Bellinzona and on to the British headquarters at Wil.

On 25 September 1944, Richard and Norman Haw left Arosa in Switzerland. They travelled through Italy and Egypt and arrived home in South Africa on 2 February the following year. [2]

In the first months of 1944 many of the liberation committees in the northern Italian cities were rounded up by the Germans and Fascists, including the main one in Milan. Giuseppe Bacciagaluppi was betrayed by a colleague and arrested by the Gestapo on 4 April. The engineer was imprisoned in the San Vittore gaol in Milan, but managed to escape three months later and to follow one of the escape routes to Switzerland.

The Milan Network continued to locate escapers and evaders and to provide them with food and shelter, but more had to be done at a local level. The number of successful evacuations fell significantly. By now over half the train parties were being intercepted and the escapers and guides arrested. A three kilometre wide area on the border had also been cleared of all of its inhabitants. Finally, the successful Allied offensive in central Italy during the summer months encouraged the hope that friendly forces would soon also overrun the north.

Giuseppe Bacciagaluppi joined the dissident Italian community in Lugano and worked for Allied intelligence and the escape and evasion secret services. These activities finally led to his arrest by the Swiss in January 1945, but he escaped in mysterious circumstances and crossed into liberated France. Bacciagaluppi returned to Italy and worked for the Allied Screening Commission, at first in Rome and then in Milan following the liberation.

In his final report, Giuseppe Bacciagaluppi revealed that there were 359 agents, sub-agents and occasional helpers in the organisation. Communists were only involved as local agents or casual operatives.

Altogether the partisan assistance service is credited with enabling 1,865 Allied servicemen to reach Switzerland, 1,297 from the British Commonwealth, 313 Yugoslavs and 255 others.

The Italians paid dearly for this major contribution to the campaign: 11 were executed or killed in action, including both of Bacciagaluppi's successors, 26 were deported to concentration camps in Germany, of whom 9 never returned, and 48 were imprisoned in Italy.

The Allied Screening Commission recommended Giuseppe Bacciagaluppi for the award of the OBE. The agency's first commandant, William Simpson, described him as 'extraordinarily courageous and brilliant.' Ulisse Cantoni was nominated for the MBE, his case described as 'especially deserving.' However, as we shall see, all such honours to Italian citizens were blocked by the British Government and establishment in 1947.

* * *

The long and difficult journey south was also only practicable because of the help of numerous Italian civilians and members of the Resistance along the way.

Fortunately, the Allied offensive in the summer of 1944 and the German withdrawal to the Gothic Line greatly reduced the length of the escape route. Liberated Florence was only 257 kilometres from Piacenza, for example, whereas Naples had been 763 kilometres away, and even Rome was 546 kilometres distant. A major effort was made to evacuate the remaining escapers and evaders in northern Italy.

Charles Macintosh, head of a new Special Force Tactical Headquarters (TAC HQ), established near Florence in November 1944, reported that:

> The daring young Italians we used as couriers through the lines became so self-assured that they would not only carry operational and intelligence reports but were soon leading parties of ex POWs and airmen, who having bailed out over enemy territory had been collected and sheltered by the partisans. [3]

Special Force, the Italian offshoot of Britain's Special Operations Executive, made a substantial contribution to the success of 'lighthouse operations,' the sheltering and bringing across the lines of Twelfth United States Army Air Force aircrew. The commanding officer, Brigadier General Charles T Meyers, had placed a B-25 Mitchell light bomber at the disposal of TAC HQ, officially for supply operations to airforce personnel protected by Special Force missions. At the end of the war, the general commended the work undertaken by Major Macintosh and his Operations Officer, Captain James Beatt:

> With a keen understanding of the problems which faced distressed airmen in enemy-occupied Italy, Major Macintosh and Captain Beatt enthusiastically directed their agents and facilities in the field to harbour and guide these airmen through enemy lines with comfort and speed. In addition, on three occasions they cooperated closely with

the Escape and Evasion Section of Twelfth Air Force in the evacuation by air of Allied military personnel from enemy territory.

Their constant interest and cooperation added to the early return of airmen from enemy-occupied Italy, which contributed immeasurably to the high morale of Air Force personnel who often readily found assistance and comfort upon forced landings in enemy territory.

The area to the north of the Gothic Line was split between nine Special Force missions. Three in Modena, Reggio and Parma were controlled by the national base at Monopoli. The other operations were located in Bologna and the Apennines and were run by Major Macintosh and TAC HQ.

One mission led by an escaper partisan from PG 29 Veano had been overrun by the enemy. In August 1944, Major Tony Oldham, DSO, MC, had been elected leader of the Lunese Division of more than 3,000 men in the Garfagnana region. Over the next five months the division carried out 50 major sabotage actions and for a time even occupied Carrara. However, on Boxing Day the new Fascist Army launched its only large-scale offensive of the war in the area. The Italian *Alpini Monte Rosa* Division and units of the German SS 16th Panzer Grenadiers retook Barga from the American 92nd Infantry Division and occupied both banks of the River Serchio north of Lucca. Major Oldham's force was obliged to cross into Allied-held territory.

The most westerly mission was led by Major Gordon Lett, an Australian-born regular officer serving with the East Surrey Regiment. Like Tony Oldham he escaped from Veano, formed his own partisan group and was appointed British Liaison Officer in the field. His operation was codenamed Blundell and was based in the Rossano Valley, in the commune of Zeri, province of Massa-Carrara, northern Tuscany. The mission is the best documented. As well as the usual reports in the National Archives at Kew, there is the fine memoir by Gordon Lett, DSO, entitled *Rossano, An Adventure of the Italian Resistance*, published in 1955. In the original foreword by the novelist Freya Stark she refers to his 'qualities of unselfish leadership ... without which the epic of the valley could never have been lived nor its history written.'

Major Lett and two 'other ranks' escapers arrived in Rossano in late September 1943. They intended to link up with Allied

Forces, but the absence of landings in the north and the slow advance in the south led them to go to ground. After talks with two Italian Army officers sent by the Genoese Resistance the Major formed his International Battalion of partisans. It was composed of Commonwealth escapers, local Italians, and Poles, Russians, Danes, Frenchmen and Yugoslavs, many of whom had escaped from ships in Genoa harbour or from *Todt* forced labour detachments. The unit began to launch attacks on garrisons, roads, electric supplies and telephone lines.

On May Day 1944, a trio of Italian A Force agents from Corsica arrived in the valley after a fraught landing near Monterosso. The mission was codenamed London. Gordon Lett recalled:

> The War Office in London had ordered that British prisoners of war were not to remain behind in Italy unless they were on special duty ... A Force Mission 'London' decided that our base would be a suitable rallying point for all escaped prisoners they might discover in the mountainous regions south of Genoa and the Po Valley. The International Battalion was given the responsibility of allotting safe houses and providing guides for them to the sea coast. [4]

A first pickup was attempted a month later. However, the shore of the *Cinque Terre* was lit by a sudden thunderstorm and the rescue craft was forced to flee under heavy fire from the garrison at Monterosso.

A second A Force mission arrived in the valley on 27 July. Major Lett heard over their radio that he had been made a British Liaison Officer at the head of Special Force Mission Blundell. Its duties were to assist in the collection and evacuation of escapers and evaders and to gather intelligence, support partisan attacks, obtain supplies and assist special operations. Another escaped prisoner of war, Lieutenant Geoffrey Lockwood, became the major's assistant, liasing with the A Force agents and with Gino and Guglielmo Cacchioli, leaders of the Beretta Brigades located near the start of the escape corridor in the Taro Valley.

The Blundell Mission was assigned two radio operators, codenamed Alfonso and Bianchi. They were sent to secure positions with the partisans in the Taro Valley. One of Major Lett's two companions in the escape from Veano, his countryman Sergeant Bob Blackmore, was active with this group, until he went through the lines to Florence early in the winter of 1944. The other escaper, the Maltese John Micallef of the Rifle Brigade, formed a group to gather intelligence and led escapers through the mountains. The rifleman eventually also crossed the lines with a report of the battalion's activities. He made contact with American forces near Pietrasanta. Micallef was sent to Naples for debriefing and was awarded the Military Medal for his work with the partisans.

In July 1944, the International Battalion joined the other formations in the newly created Fourth Partisan Zone. This was overseen by the La Spezia Committee of Liberation and commanded from Adelano by an Italian officer, Colonel Mario Fontana. The mission was attached to his headquarters for liaison with the Allies.

One of the most important functions was the arranging of parachute drops of weapons and supplies. First attempts were unsuccessful owing to technical problems and enemy action. While the American OSS showered neighbouring formations with everything they needed it was November 1944 before the battalion received its first airlift - and then it only consisted of antique blunderbusses and some sacks of dried potatoes. A shot-down American airman was speedily sent through the lines with an urgent request for modern weapons. Future drops were more effective and at the turn of the year began to be carried out in daylight.

In November, TAC HQ had made direct contact with the mission. Major Macintosh sent one of his top Italian agents through the lines to obtain a detailed report from Major Lett and to deliver 100,000 lire in notes. At age twenty-one, Lieutenant Gambarotta was already a twice-wounded veteran of the Russian campaign and an experienced partisan. He told the commander that a letter of introduction would not be enough to establish his identity, adding, 'Major Lett and the partisan leaders will require something more. Their whole area is thick with enemy spies and this note could have been taken by the Germans and handed over to one of their agents.'

Major Macintosh left the room and returned minutes later with a package. He said: 'Give him this and you will be accepted.'

Three days later, Major Lett read the note, asked for further proof and was given the object. He recalled:

The wrapping removed, it revealed a bottle of Scotch whisky. For a moment I gazed at it in silent wonder. The label seemed authentic. I called the colonel and we opened it with reverence. There was no doubt that it was the real thing. Gambarotta could not have been provided with a better passport. [5]

The lieutenant left next day with the situation report. He collected dispatches from the mission in Parma before returning to Florence a week later. From this time, overall responsibility for the escape line passed from MI 9 to SOE, from IS 9 to Special Force. To the partisans and Allied agents who ran the service it became known as *la ferrovia*, the railway, an echo of the 'underground railroad' for runaway slaves in nineteenth century America.

The route ran from the plains of western Emilia to the Apuan Alps in northern Tuscany and through the Gothic Line. From Rossano the escapers crossed the mountains to the neighbouring valley of Calice. Guides were provided by Lieutenant Daniele Bucchioni who organised the southern leg of the journey. The trip lasted a week or more, depending on the weather conditions and enemy activity on the front line. The fugitives were taken along the mountain ridge and into the valley of the Magra. After a river crossing, the route lay through the village of Fosdinovo and into the white marble mountains of Carrara. It was a difficult climb. After passing Vinca the trail reaches a height of 6,500 feet. There are splendid views of the sea. On the edge of the mountains, guides used caves and quarries to hide the men from German patrols. There was the danger of mines and hidden machine gun posts. An ancient mule track then took the escapers straight down to the Allied-held town of Seravezza on the plain.

There is a fine account of an escape along the line in the book, *From Capri into Oblivion*, by British naval officer and SOE agent Lieutenant Commander Adrian Gallegos. He spent 13 months as a prisoner and escaper in Germany and Austria as well as Italy. One of the officer's companions on the journey from Rossano was Lieutenant Jack Younger of the Coldstream Guards who had been at PG 49 Fontanellato. Their party of nine men and one woman crossed American forward positions on 20 October 1944.

Adrian Gallegos was instructed to go on leave to London. He was interviewed there by the Joint Intelligence Committee and wrote later: 'Both with General Ismay and with Sir Desmond

Morton, secretary to the Prime Minister, I pleaded the case of the partisans who, I considered, were not receiving the full measure of support they deserved.' Adrian Gallegos returned to Italy and became Major Charles Macintosh's second in command at TAC HQ.

Christmas-time saw the transit along the line of an 18-man section from the United States OSS Operational Group Mission Walla Walla. The special forces were led by Captain William Wheeler and had been dropped in Liguria in August to assist the partisans of the Sixth Zone. The party had been ordered to withdraw in face of the great enemy offensive, which within days would also engulf the valley.

As well as Allied personnel, the freedom trail was followed by members of the Resistance and by deserters from the Fascist and German armies. By the end of the war an estimated 800 men had used the route.

On 27 December, the British SAS parachuted into Rossano. The day before, base had received a message from the field that Major Lett had been murdered. His radio had broken down and so no checks could be made. The commander of the mission, Captain Bob Walker Brown, who was a friend of the major's from Chieti, decided to go ahead with the operation. A Special Force agent and a wireless operator were dropped first to see if the reception was friendly.

Captain Christopher Leng was greeted by Major Lett on the snow-covered drop zone. A Very light pistol was fired to signal the all clear and the descent began. It was the largest daylight airlift undertaken for Special Force in the campaign so far. More than 300 coloured parachutes bearing men and supplies drifted down to the valley from seven Douglas Dakota C-47s. Unfortunately, one of the planes involved in a further supply drop on 30 December became caught in an air pocket and hit the mountain side with the loss of all seven American airmen on board.

The mission, codenamed Operation Gallia, was undertaken by First Troop 3 Squadron 2 SAS. The aim was 'to attack the enemy lines of communication used by the 148th German Infantry Division, with a view if possible to making them withdraw troops from the line in order to secure their communications.' The SAS engaged roving enemy patrols and launched raids along the coastal road between La Spezia and Genoa and in the Magra Valley.

40

On 10 February, at the conclusion of the mission, Captain Bob Walker Brown wrote, 'A B-25 dropped operational money and comforts. It was then decided to begin withdrawing towards the Allied lines, carrying out a small number of attacks on the way.' The SAS followed the escape route in two columns. They scaled Monte Altissimo at night and at 0400 hours on 15 February crossed American forward positions. The mission was judged 'remarkably successful' by Major Roy Farran, commander of 3 Squadron in Italy.

On 15 March, one of the last parties to use the escape line included Major Lett and Captain Leng. In view of the impending Allied offensive it was time for the officers to be reassigned. Lieutenant Lockwood had carried a report to Florence at the end of February and on 6 March a relief Special Force mission had been parachuted into Rossano led by Major Henderson. The orders were to liase with and assist the command of the Fourth Zone, pass on the directives of the 15th Army Group, and collect and communicate intelligence to headquarters.

The journey south took ten days. After crossing the River Magra a guide conducted Gordon Lett and his companions across the mountains to a rendezvous with a Special Force agent who escorted them through the enemy lines. The group met American troops on the outskirts of Barga.

The major led the first of small Special Force forward parties chosen to liase between the advancing Fifth Army and the partisans. The 'all out' order was given to Major Henderson on 10 April and the partisans attacked garrisons, roads, barracks and fuel depots. Major Lett recrossed the lines and returned to the Fourth Zone. On 20 April, he reached the port of La Spezia, which was held by a small partisan force following a German withdrawal. The spearhead of the American 92nd Infantry Division arrived next day. On the 23rd they were joined by the mountain partisan formations under Colonel Fontana.

Major Lett was attached to the American HQ as Liaison Officer for Partisan Affairs and then became Allied Military Governor of Pontremoli. He was awarded the Italian Silver Medal for Military Valour and the British DSO for his services behind the lines.

On 6 June 1946, the Bishop of Pontremoli dedicated a memorial at Arzelato on the border to the valley. It was commissioned by Gordon Lett 'as a sign of gratitude and in recognition of all that this partisan population has suffered for the ideal of Liberty.'

From the Armistice of September 1943 to the liberation the people of the valley gave food and lodging to 440 Allied military personnel and escaped prisoners. The total was made up of 16 operatives of the British Military Mission and 50 British parachutists, together with 281 other men from the Commonwealth, 18 Americans, 3 Belgians, 4 Dutchmen, 2 Frenchmen, 32 Poles, 25 Russians and 9 Yugoslavs. [6]

*　*　*

A considerable number of partisans in the Emilia region were from families like my own who had emigrated to the United Kingdom. Ettore Arquati was born in London in 1926. When he was two-years-old his mother sent him to be cared for by his aunt in the small village of Felegara in the Commune of Medesano in the Taro Valley, south-west of Parma. At the outbreak of war, Ettore's father was interned on the Isle of Man as an enemy alien. In Italy the youth came under suspicion as a British Subject and in April 1944 he joined the partisans. He was 17-years-old.

Ettore was known by the *nome di battaglia* of Sella or by his family nickname of Ninetto. He served with the 31st and 12th Garibaldi Brigades in the Ceno and Taro valleys. The partisan base was south-west of Bardi on Monte Barigazzo (1,284 metres), midway between the two valleys. The flat mountaintop is reputed locally to be the haunt of wizards and devils.

From March 1944, the partisans were provided with weapons and supplies by Allied airdrops. On 10 June, the rebels occupied Bardi. At a public meeting in the square, lawyer Giuseppe Lumia was chosen as mayor. A committee was formed to assist Allied prisoners of war, the *Comitato Assistenziale fra gli ex prigionieri Britannici*. In his 1945 book, *Bardi, Centrale di Patriotteria*, Giuseppe Lumia related that 40 servicemen had been sheltered in the locality. The partisans gradually moved down the valley and the Free Zone of the Val Ceno was inaugurated. It covered 10 communes. On 26 June, The Free Territory of Taro was also created, with Achille Pellizzari as Prefect. The area included the mid section of the important railway line between Parma and La Spezia.

However, during the last two weeks of July a roundup conducted by the Germans and the Fascist Decima Mas extinguished both liberated sectors. Savage reprisals were taken against the local population: 40 civilians were executed, including

3 priests, and the villages of Pessola and Strela were put to the torch.

The partisans were forced to live rough. At night they walked miles across the hills in search of food and shelter. The men knew the farms where they would be made welcome and those of Fascist sympathisers that had to be avoided. The farmers did not have a lot to give and faced retribution if caught helping the Resistance. On one occasion, Ettore and his group were even turned away by a relative as there were Germans nearby.

The rebels carried out attacks on convoys and garrisons and sabotaged road and rail links. After the successful Allied summer offensive, couriers also took intelligence reports as far as the Cisa Pass. The messages were handed over to other partisans for transit through the lines and on to Allied headquarters in Florence.

On 3 September 1944, a partisan central command (*Comando Unico* or *CU*) was formed for the Province of Parma at Pian del Monte. As recounted by the former partisan Luigi Sbodio in his book, *Fornovo Taro nel Movimento Partigiano*, Ettore was appointed courier for the new headquarters. He connected with a network of messengers that carried daily letters, documents and money between partisans in the mountains and the City of Parma, and vice versa.

However, shortly after the commanders had left the area, a village girl who had been punished by the partisans for sleeping with a German informed the Fascists that Ettore was hiding in the roof of his aunt's house. He was arrested by the Black Brigade and imprisoned at Sant' Andrea Bagni. The partisans learned from an informant that Ettore was being tortured in an attempt to gain information on the clandestine activity. He was burnt with a red-hot poker, hit by a rifle butt and had his nails pulled out. Still he did not talk and was fortunate to be visited by his cousin, Don Carlo Sorenti, a young student priest, who brought him bread, salami and cigarettes concealed in his cassock.

'Meanwhile,' Luigi Sbodio recalled, 'We decided to attempt to prise our young courier from the hands of the Black Brigade and at the same time force the surrender of the garrison at Sant' Andrea.' Two members of the militia had been found who were willing to open the door of their barracks to the partisans. The raid was set for two in the morning on 25 September.

Cognome e Nome	ARQUATI ETTORE
Paternità	Giuseppe Nome di battaglia SELLA
Maternità	

Data e luogo di nascita ...... 04.11.1926   LONDRA   (GB)

Distretto di leva ...... PARMA

Nazionalità ...... ITALIANA

Domicilio ...... FELEGARA   (Parma)

Professione ...... sconosciuta

Grado nelle formazioni patriottiche ...... PARTIGIANO

Grado nelle FF. AA. ......

Formazioni patriottiche cui ha appartenuto ...... 31^ Brigata Copelli
aggregato alla Missione inglese TOFFEE

maggiore CHARLES OLLAND e capitano Michael

Tyler (Taller ?) - congedato 12^ Brigata.
Anzianità partigiana

29.04.1944   -   25.04.1945

Ferite o malattie in servizio (luogo di ricovero)

A.P.C.
Comitato Prov.le
PARMA

Partisan record card of London-born Ettore Arquati who served with the Parmesan Resistance under the *nome di battaglia* of Sella. (*Associazione Partigiani Cristiani*)

The action was going well until the unexpected appearance of the garrison commandant. He reacted angrily when challenged and there was no alternative but to shoot him. The sound echoed across the barracks and also alerted nearby Germans. The operation had to be abandoned.

Shortly afterwards, Ettore was collected from prison and driven in an open truck to Varano castle. He thought he was about to be put against a wall and shot. Instead there was a white flag in the middle of the bridge and Ettore found himself part of a prisoner exchange. A captured German major and non-commissioned officer were swapped for 20 partisans.

On 12 November, Allied aircraft bombed the German Headquarters in Sant' Andrea Bagni as a result of information supplied by the Resistance. The German commander in Italy, Field Marshal Kesselring, was paying a visit. There were many casualties, but the field marshal escaped injury and speedily left the area.

Ettore also assisted the British Special Force mission attached to *Comando Unico*, which operated in the upland area to the east of the Cisa highway. His newly discovered partisan record card reads: 'Member of the 31st Copelli Brigade, which was associated with the Toffee Mission of Major Charles Holland and Captain Michael Tyler. Part of the 12th Brigade on discharge. Served from 29 April 1944 to 25 April 1945.'

Following the liberation, the Red Cross repatriated Ettore and other partisans who had been born in the United Kingdom. The men were driven across France in a large car. Ettore complained that he was given rice pudding on the Channel ferry. He finally returned to the London he had left at age two in 1928. [7]

NOTES

[1] Escape Report in TNA: PRO WO 208/4253.

[2] Information credit: Richard Bryson, South Africa, grandson of Richard and nephew of Norman Haw. Richard's father, Private John Louis (Jack) Bryson of the Botha Regiment was also captured at Tobruk and held as a POW in Italy. However, on 9 September 1943, together with most of the prisoners at PG 52 Chiavari, he was entrained to Germany. Jack Bryson was eventually liberated by the Americans near Regensburg on 24 April 1945.

[3] Charles Macintosh, *From Cloak to Dagger*, p 109. Special Force was the popular abbreviation of No. 1 Special Force, the cover name for the Italian branch of Britain's sabotage and subversion agency, the Special Operations Executive. See my book, *Special Force: SOE and the Italian Resistance 1943-1945*.

[4] Gordon Lett, *Rossano*, new edition, pp 12-13.

[5] Ibid., p 139.

[6] Information credit: Brian Gordon Lett, Devon.

[7] Information credit: Sylvia Arquati, London. Copy of Ettore Arquati's service card kindly obtained by Dott. Sergio Giliotti of the *Associazione Partigiani Cristiani*, Parma, and Comm. Mario Trivelloni of Pontremoli.

4 THE LONG ROAD SOUTH

A few escapers and evaders aiming to link up with the Allies in southern Italy went west of the Apennines and reached American forces south of Venafro. Most though followed the eastern slopes into the high country overlooking the River Sangro. One officer escaper described the routes as forming a funnel at the southern end of the mountains a few days' march from friendly forces. As many as 6,000 Allied servicemen were said to be in the area. They shared caves and mountain huts with Italians avoiding the call up or forced labour. Most of the fugitives lacked adequate clothing and footwear for the severe winter conditions and food supplies became increasingly scarce. As the winter line stabilised the Germans were also able to deploy whole regiments to search for escapers and evaders. Many were recaptured, others were forced to give themselves up, and a few were shot.

It is time we followed the adventures of some of the men who chose to walk hundreds of miles. Twenty-five year old Lieutenant John Andrew (Jack) Comyn of the 8th King's Royal Irish Hussars was captured by the Italians on 10 December 1940. He had been promoted to tank troop commander. His vehicle was hit by enemy fire on the Sofafi Ridge, just inside Egypt, and the driver and gunner killed. It was the second day of the successful British counter-offensive. Jack Comyn was eventually driven to Tripoli and taken to Naples on board the liner *Conte Rosso*. At the time the Italians only held three other British officers.

Over the next four years and five months Jack Comyn was an inmate of six prisoner of war camps, three in Italy, PG 78 Sulmona, PG 41 Montalbo and nearby PG 49 Fontanellato, and three in Germany. While in Italy, he formed a dance band, which provided music for concerts and stage shows. At PG 49 it grew to twelve performers with Comyn on the piano. On 29 August 1943, he was promoted to captain. Jack Comyn later described Fontanellato as 'undoubtedly the most pleasant POW camp I ever encountered.' It was the only one he revisited.

After leaving the camp at midday on 9 September, the prisoners marched to the wooded, dried up watercourse of the Torrente Rovacchia, five miles north-west. The hiding place had been chosen that morning by Lieutenant Colonel Hugh Mainwaring, formerly GSO 1 (Operations) to General Montgomery, together with the Italian second in command, Captain Camino.

The valley of the Stirone torrent. To the south is Parma Province, and to the north, Piacenza and the Arda Valley. Major Sam Derry, commander of the British Organisation in Rome for Assisting Allied Escaped Prisoners of War, wrote that there had originally been 600 servicemen in the area, about half of whom made their way to Switzerland or to warmer parts of Italy.

For the next two days, Captain Comyn acted as the lieutenant colonel's staff officer and was present at anxious consultations between him and the British commander, Lieutenant Colonel Hugo De Burgh. Comyn recalled: 'The SBO considered that he had obeyed the War Office orders in that he had so far kept us all together. But it was clearly impossible to continue feeding 500 of us in the ravine, and the Germans might at any moment discover where we were.' [1] During Saturday, 11 September, orders were distributed to the companies for dispersal that evening. It was 'every man for himself.'

Lieutenant Colonel Mainwaring invited Captain Comyn to join a small group he was forming. But Comyn reluctantly decided to stay with his friends in the regiment. 'It was,' he said later, 'one of the biggest mistakes I ever made.' Mainwaring took another of his aides, a Belgian lieutenant called Leon Blanchaert, who spoke Italian fluently, and a Greek lieutenant, George Lascaris. They crossed the lines to British forces at Casacalenda on 13 October.

Jack Comyn and his friends formed a sixteen strong group of Cavalrymen and Greenjackets. They decided to make for the hills and to avoid all towns, major roads and railways. Comyn said: 'Our plan was to move west across the Via Emilia into the foothills of the Apennines and there await events.' There were constant reports that the Allies intended to make a landing at La Spezia, only 60 miles away. However, he added, 'Many months later we learned that these reports, emanating from the BBC, were put out to deceive the Germans. They certainly deceived us.'

At dusk the group left across the fields. Italian civilians emerged from the shadows with offers of clothing and help. Jack Comyn accepted civilian garments, but kept his battledress jacket in his knapsack as the penalty for being caught behind enemy lines in disguise and without proof of identity could be execution as a spy.

'The first problem was to get over the railway line and the Via Emilia,' Jack Comyn told me. 'There was quite a lot of German military traffic on the road and we had to wait for intervals to scramble across. I remember some nasty wire fences. After that we just headed west into the hills in darkness and covered about 16 miles that night.'

At 4am, the eldest of the men, Charles Hedley, complained of foot soreness, so they laid up in a wood on a hilltop.

First light revealed a small farmstead only 100 feet below. As the captain was judged the most fluent in Italian he was sent to investigate. He heard gentle noises coming from the cowshed and found the farmer on a stool milking. There was the warm smell of cows and hay and straw. 'It was,' Comyn recalled, 'a miraculous moment, in the half light of that cool fresh dawn, to find myself free and in touch again with normal human existence.' The farmer did not appear at all surprised at the intrusion and provided a pail of milk and another filled with hot water for the captain's footsore friend.

Later that morning three young Italian soldiers visited the escapers in the woods. They offered the Englishmen some of their hand grenades, but given the weapon's reputation as being more dangerous to the bearer than to any enemy, the gesture was politely declined. The Italians said that the fugitives would soon be meeting 'an English millionaire.' In his book, *Episodes,* Jack Comyn recalled:

The sun shone through the leaves, there were wild flowers and fungi, and above all there was the wonderful sensation of wandering with impunity along grassy tracks through the trees. Towards noon Signor Palumbo, the 'English millionaire,' arrived and greeted us cheerily in faultless Cockney. It transpired that he had spent over 20 years running a restaurant in Soho, and if not to our eyes an English millionaire was certainly so to his neighbours, even though his million was in Lire.

This was providential. During the next five weeks our whole existence revolved around Signor Palumbo. In Italy at that time the ownership and farming of land was based on the *mezzadria* system, by which the landowner (*padrone)* provided the capital and the farmer (*contadino*) worked the farm. No rent was paid, the produce of the land being divided equally between the *padrone* and the *contadino*. Traditional estates had always been run this way, but the system also provided an investment opportunity for those who had made good. Signor Palumbo was a *padrone*, owning several scattered farms. To these he proceeded to distribute us, approximately four to each farm.

It had anyway become obvious that 16 could not stay together. Such a number made the party too conspicuous, besides difficult to feed. Four of us, 8th Hussars, formed a group and were guided to the farm of La Trinità, the home of Ernesto Regalo. La Trinità stood high up on the south flank of the little Torrente Stirone, a *torrente* being a stream in winter, dry in summer. Ernesto Regalo, aged about forty, had a wife and young twin daughters. Above his little holding was woodland and below the farmstead the land sloped gently towards the Stirone, beside which ran a country road down the valley. [2]

The Hussars spent the next six weeks on the farm, sleeping in the hay barn and enjoying the rhythm of country life. Not only were they well looked after by the Regalo family but also every few days Signor Palumbo would send up a horse and cart loaded with flour, salami, ham, chickens, cheese and wine.

The soldiers were in order of seniority: Captain Patrick de Cleremont, the newly promoted Captain Comyn, Lieutenant Charles Hedley, the eldest, and Second Lieutenant Donald Astley-Cooper, the youngest. Rank still mattered because the men had been trained to follow the decisions of the senior officer, even in these unusual circumstances.

Patrick (Pat) Howard Voltelin de Cleremont was the flamboyant future commander of the regiment and recipient of the DSO for 'valiant and distinguished service' in Korea. Aged 33, he had been recalled from the Reserve List in 1939 and served in the Western Desert, acting as Adjutant and twice being Mentioned in Despatches. He was captured together with many other Hussars at the Battle of Sidi Rezegh in November 1941. Charles Hedley was to be a Hussar for 32 years and had already been a soldier for 25 years. He was commissioned Quartermaster in the Field in 1940 and had been captured at Bir Hakeim in May 1942. Hedley was a Lancastrian, known as 'the little man with the big smile.' He was a hard worker and an able administrator. Donald Astley-Cooper was the clarinet player in Captain Comyn's band at Fontanellato. He remembered him as a great athlete and a shy but charming young man.

In mid October the escapers held a meeting to discuss their situation. An argument developed. Captain de Cleremont insisted that they should stay put and wait until the area was overrun by Allied troops. Captain Comyn said that landings in the north were not going to take place and that they should move south. The conflict was resolved by Patrick de Cleremont and Charles Hedley remaining and Jack Comyn and Donald Astley-Cooper leaving. Comyn related: 'Pat eventually agreed to our departure. In fairness to his judgement he got home long before me.'

Captain de Cleremont and Lieutenant Hedley remained in the area for another year. My mother was among their helpers. In late October 1944, the pair moved south-west and followed the Rossano escape line. They made contact with the United States 92nd Infantry Division who promptly threw them into prison as suspected enemy agents. Fortunately, the officers escaped the firing squad and returned to England in December 1944. They went back to the regiment in time to take part in the Rhine crossing and the Victory Parade in Berlin.

Over six weeks, Jack Comyn and Donald Astley-Cooper travelled down a large part of Italy. Apart from 30 miles by train near Rome the journey was all on foot. The route lay along the north-eastern flank of the Apennines till just north of Florence, then across to the Tiber Valley, south-east to the Sabine Hills and into the Abruzzo. The walk ended within six miles of Alfedena on the River Sangro, where Allied troops halted for the winter.

The two friends relied on the *contadini* for food and shelter for all but a few days. The Hussars were given an excellent meal at the Franciscan mountaintop Sanctuary of La Verna in the Casentino Forest, but were not allowed to stay the night. The captain's boots were repaired by a cobbler monk. Three days were also spent with a genial *padrone* called Pietro Falconi at his villa in Ginestra Sabina. He organised a large cocktail party in honour of the escapers, to which he invited his friends from Rome. Falconi also took the cavalrymen riding on thoroughbred horses around his estate, oblivious of the presence of a German post a quarter of a mile away.

Only on two occasions were the walkers refused hospitality by the sometimes poverty-stricken countryfolk. Money was never offered and never requested. The Hussars would leave a note asking the Allies to recognise what their hosts had done for them.

The daily routine varied little. Jack Comyn wrote:

Every evening we would approach some lonely farmhouse, declare who we were, and ask to be received. There would be a family kitchen/living room similar to that of Ernesto Regalo. The cauldron would hang over the fire and we would sit down to the evening meal of pasta or polenta and home produced wine, very much as we had experienced at La Trinità. Food was not plentiful and we heard many complaints of the quality of the wartime grey flour and of the difficulty of getting salt. All salt in Italy came from Sicily, then occupied by the Allies. It is surprising how much its complete absence affects the taste of food.

Always the family, often very cut off from the outside world, would enquire eagerly as to where we had come from and ask for news of the war. Then the talk would turn to other topics, a favourite being the advantage of having married priests, which they understood to be the case in the Anglican Church. Where this was asked there was usually some hint of misconduct by their own. All too often the subject was the fate of their sons, far away with the Italian divisions in Russia, prisoners of war in Britain or Canada, or just missing. Many mothers told us they trusted in the Lord that if they looked after us someone would look after their own son.

It must not be thought that my Italian learned from books was always equal to these conversations. For one thing every valley seemed to have its dialect, sometimes very different to the pure Tuscan tongue. But we managed somehow.

There was one occasion when my Italian failed me badly. By mid October, when we started our journey, the weather had turned very cold by night. After supper we would always ask to sleep in the warmth of the cowshed, although we were often offered beds. By now the death penalty had been decreed for anyone harbouring ex prisoners of war. In view of this danger to our hosts we hoped that if surprised in the byre we could vow that the farmer had no knowledge of our presence on his farm. On this occasion, during a convivial evening, beds were pressed on us. I carefully explained the reason for refusing and insisted that we should sleep in the cowbyre. An hour later we were escorted there and found all the family's finest pillows, linen and blankets laid out on the stone floor behind the cows' tails. I fear that my Italian had not been good enough that evening and that our hosts must have concluded, from what I said, only that English preferences were somewhat eccentric. [3]

Captain Comyn and Second Lieutenant Astley-Cooper made good progress and by 28 November had reached the battle zone. They decided to push on through the snow until contact was made with British forces. However, after twenty-four hours the pair were forced by mist and low cloud to seek shelter in a shepherd's hut. It was near the hamlet of Opi, within the German forward area. 'We saw a figure, plainly a British soldier, coming out to collect firewood,' said Comyn, 'and could not resist the idea of a fire.' Three British soldiers were already inside the stone building and three Sikhs joined them later. Suddenly there was the rattle of automatic fire and a shout, 'Look out, the Jerries are coming!' The 'other ranks' fled, but were soon rounded up. Comyn and Astley-Cooper hid in a storeroom. They were rumbled when the German officer noticed the discrepancy between the number of captives and the hats and knapsacks left lying around. An axe suddenly shattered a boarded up window of the hiding place. A large, round, bespectacled German face looked in. *'Raus!'* (out) was all he said. The patrol of front-line troops had seen the smoke and decided to investigate. Jack Comyn recalled:

> It was the most miserable point in my life. Having got hold of us, we were marched practically all day down the mountains. I just remember being exhausted and terribly hungry to the point of hallucinating. Our journey had begun near Piacenza in the north and we had got to the south of Rome ... It was horrifying to find oneself a prisoner of war again after such an effort. [4]

The men were placed in a POW compound and later entrained for Moosburg in southern Germany. [5]

* * *

Jack Comyn often contrasted his ordeal with the success of his friend, Major Hugh Hope, MC, of the King's Royal Rifle Corps (KRRC). In *Episodes*, Comyn wrote:

> Our experiences in the mountains did not endear us to that route but it was perfectly practicable. A week or two before we tried to get through, my friend Hugh Hope had, travelling alone, taken a similar course to ours and walked into Alfedena without encountering either a German or British patrol. His first sight of our troops in that little town was of a British soldier sitting in a barber's shop having his hair cut. [6]

54

Jack Comyn told me: 'Hugh Hope set off south on his own, speaking no Italian, and got through the lines successfully! His farm was within half a mile of La Trinità, on the same side of the Stirone.' Also there was Lieutenant Derek Hornsby, another KRRC officer from Fontanellato. The servicemen in the area met frequently, after dark. [7]

Major Hope, a regular soldier from Midlothian, had been captured at Sidi Rezegh on 21 November 1941 together with the rest of the 1st Battalion, KRRC, in the 7th Armoured Division. The officer was involved in escape attempts at all three of his camps, Sulmona, Montalbo and Fontanellato. He also distracted an Italian sergeant during Comyn's unsuccessful bid to leave PG 49 disguised as a building worker. [8] Major Hope's Escape Report reads:

On 9 September 1943 on the approach of the Germans to the camp we were released by the Italians and all the 500 officers laid up near the camp. I then went off with two others, Lieutenant Paul O' Brien-Swayne and Lieutenant Derek Hornsby (now in Switzerland), both KRRC. On 15 September, we split and from then on I was alone. I was sheltered by a farmer at Aione near Borla. The farm opposite was raided and a Yugoslav captain captured, so I decided to leave. I was given civilian clothes by my helpers.

I walked south down the Apennines from 18 October till 21 November, when I was near Castel di Sangro. During my walk I had to give my watch - a Rolex Oyster which cost me £10 before the war - in order to get my boots resoled, the Italian refusing to accept local currency. Near Pescara I met an American parachutist officer who had been arranging the evacuation of ex prisoners of war by sea. The scheme had come to an end by this time.

I crossed the Sangro River near Castel di Sangro and reached the British lines at first light on 21 November. I was sent to HQ 13 Corps where I had a tactical interrogation. From there I went back on a personal visit to an officer in my regiment at Vasto. Here I met General Montgomery who said I could stay in Italy and go to the 2nd Battalion of my regiment. [9].

Jack Comyn revisited the Stirone Valley in 1984. He recalled:

La Trinità was by then an abandoned ruin, like so many hill farms in Italy. Ernesto and his wife, both much aged, had a small modern house with a patch of vineyard in Borla. He opened a bottle of wine and we talked. One of the twins was married, the other a nurse in Swansea. He told me that they had looked after many other escapees after my departure. I had an uncomfortable feeling that of me he had little recollection, although he clearly remembered Hugh Hope who had been to see him soon after the war. [10]

NOTES

[1] John Andrew (Jack) Comyn, *Episodes*, pp 88-9.
[2] Ibid., pp 91-2.
[3] Ibid., pp 97-8.
[4] Patrick Wilson, *The War Behind the Wire*, p 108.
[5] Sadly, Donald Astley-Cooper was killed in action on 3 January 1951 while serving as a captain with the regiment in Korea.
[6] Comyn, op. cit., p 113.
[7] Information credit: I was fortunate to be in contact with Major Comyn in Somerset when researching my first book. After a career in farming in Eire and Essex he retired in 1980 and followed his other great interests, writing and fishing.
[8] See *Episodes*, pp 83-4. The story is retold on page 31 of my book, *British Prisoners of War in Italy: Paths to Freedom*.
[9] Escape Report in TNA: PRO WO 208/3318.
[10] Comyn, op. cit., p 96.

5 ESCAPE TO SWITZERLAND

Allied escapers arrived on the Swiss frontier within days of the Armistice. A group of 70 prisoners of war was admitted at Chiasso on 22 September 1943. Most of the men were 'Free French' or Cypriots from 'other ranks' camp PG 62 Grumello del Piano, near Bergamo, which was thrown open by the Italians. However, the news that thousands more Allied servicemen were on their way led to delays on the border as crisis talks were held in Bern. Eventually the British Government agreed to the Swiss exercising a measure of military control over the fugitives, though under International Law prisoners of war escaping from capture into neutral territory were free men. Following this gentleman's agreement, Allied escapers and evaders were freely admitted to the Confederation.

The servicemen were largely confined to villages in the cantons of St Gallen and Thurgau in the north-east of the country and Swiss troops were stationed in the billeting areas. A British headquarters was established at Wil in St Gallen. The Swiss called the internees *évadés*, though evaders in the British sense of servicemen who avoided capture while in enemy-held territory were held in military camps.

Allied escapers usually made for one of three Swiss salients into Italian territory. The Italian helpers preferred the most central and direct route. It ran from Milan to the border crossing at Chiasso, a journey of only 51 kilometres, around an hour by train. As controls became stricter on the Italian side of the frontier a new escape corridor was opened up. The rail journey ended on the Milan to Tirano mainline along the eastern side of Lake Como at stations such as Lecco, Varenna, Bellano and Colico. Servicemen were taken across the lake by boat or ferry to the western shore and guided over the mountains to the Ticino Canton of Switzerland.

The two other main routes went through less populous, remote areas and were not so reliant on public transport. These pathways were increasingly used. By the spring of 1944 more than half the escorted rail journeys were coming to grief, with the arrest of all the escapers and guides.

The first New Zealander escapers from PG 106 Vercelli arrived in Switzerland on 19 September 1943. About half the others eventually followed, accounting for 70 per cent of the 108 New Zealand servicemen in the country. [1] Most went over the Monte

British escapers on a Swiss farm. On the right is Rifleman Ransome (Rannie) Dawson from Lancashire. He was captured in North Africa while serving with the Parachute Regiment. The rifleman was held in Italy at PG 59 Servigliano and at work camp 20 of PG 146 Mortara, from where he made his escape on the Armistice. (Kydd)

Moro pass to the north-east of Monte Rosa. This westerly route ran over the mountains to the north of Biella, east down to Alagna at the head of the Sesia Valley, over the ridge to Macugnaga in the Ansasca Valley, then west over the 10,000 foot pass and down a glacier to the village of Almagell in Switzerland.

One party retained their uniforms for the whole journey. A member of the group related that their appearance caused a sensation in the village of Alagna. They were given a wooden hut in which to spend the night. The journey involved a great deal of rock climbing and some dangerous drops, but by using refuges and employing guides the men eventually reached the border. Swiss troops were already there. 'They seemed to be waiting for us,' recalled one escaper.

The eastern option was equally as hazardous, as becomes clear in this fine account of his time as a prisoner of war by John Muir of Glasgow:

> I volunteered to join the Army on Monday, 4 September 1939, and after training received my commission as a 2nd Lieutenant in the Durham Light Infantry at the end of April 1940. I joined the 1st Battalion in the Mersa Matruh fortress in Egypt in August as a Platoon Commander in C Company.
>
> I was on detachment to the 7th Armoured Division throughout Wavell's massive victory over the Italian Army during December 1940 to March 1941. I rejoined the battalion at Qassassin, near Suez. The unit was in 2 Brigade with 3rd Coldstream Guards and 2nd Scots Guards, preparing for an amphibious landing on an island in the Dodecanese.
>
> In mid April the brigade was rushed up to the frontier between Egypt and Libya to stem Rommel's advance. After various engagements an operation named Brevity was launched, and brief it was, a dawn attack and a dusk withdrawal. C Company, with D Company in reserve, captured the objective of Fort Capuzzo with considerable losses.
>
> I was wounded during the afternoon and when the Germans counter-attacked early in the evening I was captured by a Panzer Light Infantry unit. After treatment at a German field hospital I was taken by Italians to a military hospital in Benghazi. After six or seven days, I joined another officer from my battalion, Neil Ritchie, a Rhodesian

serving in the RAF, Hugh Baker, and an Australian infantry officer, Trevor Neuendorf.

We were moved by stages to a POW camp at Tarhuna, lying to the south of Tripoli. After two or three weeks we were on the move again, first by ship over the Mediterranean, then by train from Naples to PG 17 Rezzanello, near Piacenza. However, on arrival we were told that there were six officers too many for the number of beds. The Commandant wanted to get rid of two of the originals, Duggie Clarke and Johnnie Birbeck, so four volunteers were required. I thought that being outside a camp gave the best chance of escape, so I was one of the six who set off by train for PG 78 Sulmona - no escape opportunity arose. I was in the first hut in the lower compound.

Towards the end of 1941 some of us were given permission by the Escape Committee to start a tunnel from the toilet area. After cutting through the concrete floor we dug a 20-foot shaft and tunnelled about 35 yards under the road running outside the camp. We had about 10 yards to go to reach a suitable place at which we could ascend when one afternoon the Italians rushed in, went straight to the toilet area and lifted the trap door leading to the shaft. I was working at the face at the time but was allowed to crawl out before being taken to the Commandant and put in a cell for the night. This was about April 1942.

In May, I was transferred with other POWs to a camp in the monastery at Padula, PG 35. I soon found a potential escape route but was refused permission by the Escaping Officer, possibly because someone else had applied. This may have been an attempt by Jack Pringle and Alastair Cram, as described in Jack's book, *Last Stop Colditz.*

A month later I was told that I was being sent to PG 5, a punishment camp for *pericolosi* [dangerous prisoners] at Gavi, near Alessandria, north-west of Genoa. This was the 'Italian Colditz,' whose inmates had made at least one previous escape attempt. I rejoined Hugh Baker and Trevor Neuendorf and shared a cell with them, another Rhodesian, two New Zealanders and an Englishman.

Early in the winter we worked out a scheme to take us to a part of the fortress that could not be reached or even seen from the POWs' section. We took our plan to Brigadier

Clifton. It was agreed, but postponed, so we knew that there was another scheme under way. This was a complex and arduous escape undertaken by South Africans, assisted by David Stirling the founder of the SAS and others including Jack Pringle and Alastair Cram, as mentioned in Jack's book. There is a very good report and a description of the fortress in *The Times* newspaper of 14 December 1945. The actual breakout was on the night of 24 and 25 April, but there was no successful escape.

After a period to allow things to settle we were given permission to start our scheme at the end of June. It involved the lifting of the metal platform in the toilets, digging into the unused dungeons which we knew lay below the row of cells and seeing where we could go. It took about a month to remove the platform (using razor blades to separate the metal from the concrete with a minimum sign of tampering) and dig down along the sewage pipe through the roof into the dungeon. We were disappointed to find that the walls at the back and far end of the vault were the solid rock on which the fortress was built. The other side wall had a bricked up doorway. We removed enough bricks to get into a passageway, but found another door and a walkway that was in constant use by the Italians. This left us with the front wall of the dungeon. We removed three heavy stones and started to tunnel under the courtyard of our cell compound towards the outer wall of the fortress.

We had gone only seven or eight feet by 8 September 1943 when an Armistice between the Allies and the Italians was announced by the Camp Commandant. Both he and Brigadier Clifton made it clear that we were to remain in the fortress until arrangements were made for our handing over to the Allies. However, the next morning we were wakened by gunfire as the Italian ration party was ambushed. Most were killed with only a few escaping back to the fortress. They were closely followed by a German SS unit, which took over. Three days later we were told to pack and be ready to move next morning. Our cell together with the brigadier, David Stirling and others involved in the earlier escape went into the dungeon we had found.

We heard the roll call next morning and the prisoners marching out. The Germans rushed about with a great deal of shouting, hammering and bashing well into the evening.

On the third day about 3pm the hammering and bashing was at our 'back door' - the bricked up one at the end of the passage leading into the Italian area. We heard German voices in the corridor. They went away but returned an hour later and knocked down the door into the dungeon. The German captain was delighted that he had found all the missing prisoners, 58 in all. Indeed he had found an extra one because two prisoners who had been in hospital had returned on the 8th but were not re-entered on the Italian lists. Either the Germans miscounted or a prisoner was still hiding. The captain told the brigadier that he had located the plan of the fortress and this had helped him find the hiding places, including our dungeon. They never discovered our entrance, but I don't suppose they bothered to look for it. We were locked up that night but next day allowed to gather some kit from our cells. We had taken off our boots while in the dungeon. Some were brought up by the Germans, but not mine. I found another pair with which I had to make do, but they were not the right size and gave me much pain later.

The next day we were marched out of what had been our home for 15 months, loaded into buses and driven away with a massive escort of German Military Police in trucks and on motorcycles with sidecars. We stopped at Mantua, where we were bedded down on the football pitch with guards all round the terracing. Next afternoon we were taken to a railway siding and packed into trucks. Hugh and I were separated from our cellmates, which I learned after the war was just as well as they were in a steel truck whereas we were in a wooden one.

The train did not move until dusk. We started cutting a hole in the front of the truck and had just finished making it big enough to squeeze through when the train stopped at Verona. We had an agonising half-hour holding a blanket over the hole while the German guards walked up and down outside. We had drawn lots in pairs and Hugh and I were 3 and 4. After the train left Verona 1 and 2 climbed out and jumped. Hugh went through the hole and I followed to find that he had gone forward onto the buffers of the next truck. This was a mistake as it meant that his leap was at best sideways, if not a little backwards, whereas mine was forwards. There had been shooting outside the train, thought to be guards discouraging escape, so we arranged to lie still until the train passed. How glad I was to see the red lights on the last carriage disappear.

I don't know what happened to numbers 1 and 2 who left before us or if any of the other 20 from our truck got away. None arrived in Switzerland. We heard later that on the night we jumped someone had been killed when escaping from a train about 20 miles farther up the line but could not get any more detail. It was rumoured that he had hit a signal.

I returned to find Hugh and we went down from the railway embankment through some scrub to find a river in front of us. Before we could do anything there was a rattling in the undergrowth and out burst an Italian soldier who took one look at us and turned and rushed back. We decided immediately to go in the opposite direction across the river. In the moonlight it looked very placid, but after wading a few steps we were carried away and swimming hard to keep afloat and make progress. We reached the other side, but at least a half-mile downstream. We learned later that this was the Adige River flowing from the Dolomites down the Trento Valley. It was only when we came out of the water that we recognised the extent of our injuries. The palms of my hands were badly grazed, my knees were scraped and I had a very sore chest, which must have taken much of the impact on landing as my pullover was ripped down the front. Hugh was in a worse condition, with hands and knees scraped and a twisted knee on one leg and a twisted ankle on the other. We were soaking wet and cold.

We set off up a slope with me helping Hugh who was walking with difficulty and in great pain. Soon we came to a vineyard. At the top there were bushes about six feet in height with branches reaching almost to the ground. We crawled in, huddled together and fell asleep. Next morning we found that the scrub was quite extensive, so we went in deeper, took off our clothes and found breaks where the sun came through to dry them and to heat ourselves. I went into the vineyard and picked bunches of grapes which we ate along with some chocolate we had. We took turns to sleep and then dressed to move at dusk, only to find that Hugh's knee and ankle were very swollen, the ankle so much so that he couldn't put his boot on that foot. We discussed the dilemma and decided that Hugh who spoke fair Italian would go to an isolated house nearby to seek help. I would take him down but hide outside so that I could go on my way if no help was available. After ten minutes of anxiety Hugh came to the door and called me in. He told me that the daughter of the house knew some Yugoslav escapers and had gone to fetch them. Meantime the woman was bathing Hugh's hands and knees, applying an ointment and wrapping them in cloths. She did the same for me and then made us coffee.

Suddenly there was a commotion and six or seven burly and noisy Slavs burst into the room. There was a great deal of handshaking and two of them picked up Hugh and took him out of the house. I too was hustled out. Hugh was placed on the shoulders of a big fellow who set off down the road followed by about 20 others, all shouting and singing. We rushed into a small village and onto a hall where they were staying. The Yugoslavs wanted to go on partying, and one who spoke a little English to go on talking, but by now it was 2am and we were exhausted, especially Hugh as the manhandling he had received worsened his original injuries. We fell asleep and it was midday before we woke.

During the afternoon there was a lot of talk. Hugh reported that the Slavs intended to move away and that the Italians had arranged to take care of us. At dusk four Italians arrived with a handcart into which they loaded Hugh and off we went into Avio, where we settled into a bedroom in the house of Emilio. I don't know his surname but think that he was an official of the town administration. Our wounds were dressed again with the same ointment, which was most soothing and effective. It was great to be in a proper bed for the first time since my leave period in Alexandria in March 1941.

Next day we had an unpleasant surprise in the arrival of the advance party of a German unit requisitioning accommodation, including the bedroom we were in. This led to feverish activity by our host and other Italians, resulting in our being moved out in the early hours of the morning with Hugh mounted on a donkey. We were taken to a cave in the hills to the east of the town, which had been set up with a flooring of branches and shrubs, covered with tarpaulin, sheets and blankets. We lived in the cave until 28 September with food brought up regularly. On the 26th we had a party for Hugh's birthday with Emilio, Maria, Lino and Aurelio. By now Hugh's knee and ankle were much less swollen and he could walk a short distance but could still not get his boot on.

During 28 September the German unit moved out. Late in the evening we were brought down from our cave to Lino's house. We stayed until 2 October, when we moved to Aurelio's. Hugh was now able to wear his boot and we were taking a walk after dark each night. We had been provided with Italian clothing and a 1932 road map so we were keen to get on our way. We left letters with all our Italian friends addressed to the British authorities advising of the great help we had received.

At 5.30am on 5 October we were given a fond farewell and newly baked bread and some cheese. Our intention was to get to Lake Garda, steal a boat in which to cross the lake, take to the hills and head for an address in Como where we knew we would get help. We started on the road northwards from Avio, but towards 9 it was busy so we took a track into the hills. This was hard on Hugh's knee and ankle, but it was a lovely sunny day so we had many stops. Towards dusk and fairly high up we came upon an isolated farm which seemed a suitable place to stop for the night. Hugh, having been educated in South Africa, spoke Afrikaans, so we decided to say that we were Dutch seamen who had left a ship at Venice and wanted to get home. Hugh spoke to me in Afrikaans and I replied with one or two words which he taught me, but mostly in grunts or shakes or nods of the head. We went to the door and Hugh told his story to an elderly woman. She was joined by her husband and Hugh repeated the tale. I don't know if it was believed or not, but we were invited in. We were given a meal of polenta and bread and cheese, then shown into a barn with a hayloft where we each spent two hours on watch and two hours asleep until 6am. We were given a cup of coffee and more bread and off we went on a track running at a good height along the west side of the valley.

About midday the trail started to go down towards a road leading into a town, so we knew that we had come too far north. We went back up the track and found another one heading west, which climbed steeply and then levelled off. I don't know how we missed it before. The path ran parallel with a ridge, which stopped after a short distance, giving us a view of Lake Garda. It was lovely in the sunshine. However we were looking down on Torbole, which was not a lovely sight as it was full of Germans - it seemed to be a HQ of some sort, but we didn't wait to see. We retreated the way we had come and then went through the town of Nago and onto a track running beside a river that was flowing towards Lake Garda. The trail rejoined the road, which led to a bridge into the town of Arco.

As there were a lot of people crossing the bridge we decided to do so too, but having set out along the road we saw that there was a German sentry at the far end. He wasn't checking papers and didn't seem to be interested in passers by. It might have been more conspicuous if we had turned round and gone back up the road, so with at least my heart in my mouth, we moved onto and over the bridge. I had difficulty in keeping an even pace and not breaking into a run after passing the sentry. More problems faced us as it turned out that Arco was a hospital town. There were red crosses all around and many wounded soldiers. My worries were increased by Hugh's decision to buy a newspaper in a shop full of German wounded. According to him he wanted to see how the war was getting on.

Arco proved to be a large town and by dusk we were still not clear of houses. There were very few people around and we urgently required shelter. We thought we might need to go to ground in a garden but then came to a monastery and were given asylum for one night only. We received bread and water and a bed that was rock hard. We left next morning as soon as there were people about.

Having concluded that Como was out of the question we decided to try for Switzerland at its nearest point (near Tirano) especially as the area ahead did not seem to be heavily populated. Little did we realise this was because it was so mountainous, as we soon found out. Worse still all the valleys were at right angles to our route.

That day, 7 October, we started climbing very soon after leaving Arco, following a bad path and taking it very slowly. When we reached the top there was a flat area with First World War trenches facing north - presumably Italian. We didn't see any Austrian trenches, so these were either in reserve, for training, or as a memorial. They were very complete, with firing steps, revetments and dugouts. It was late afternoon when we got down into the next valley. We sought out an isolated farm, told our tale, and were given a meal of cheese and potatoes baked beside the fire, and a bed in the hayloft. We were so exhausted that there was no question of taking turns on watch - we both slept and were only wakened when the farmer went off to work about 7am. We left without breakfast, as none was offered, and climbed about 2,000 feet over a saddle and down to a valley. We walked along a road, crossed a river by a bridge which was unguarded, climbed again, and then down to the village of Brione, which we reached in the early afternoon. We were greeted by a tremendous lightning display with thunder and torrential rain.

The rain was so heavy we had to get shelter as soon as possible. We went to a house set apart from the others and told our tale to the lady who opened the door. She was joined by her husband who invited us in. He provided us with towels and some clothing and took away our garments to dry them. We were given a good meal with wine. During the evening it became clear that our Dutch sailor story was not believed and that they knew we were escaped POWs. We had to agree and were told that they would help us on our way. They gave us some extra clothing and a more up to date and large-scale map. I regret that I cannot remember their surname. We slept in the living room and the next day they sent their son, Silvio, aged about 13, to guide us on our next stage. He was a lovely boy and we were sorry when he left us about midday.

During this day we had two climbs and two dropdowns into valleys and finally a further climb through a forest where again the rain started. We came across a woodcutter's hut with a charcoal fire, which we huddled over to dry our clothes. The woodcutter was not very pleased to find us there but gave us a cup of coffee and some cheese.

Next day after a further short climb through the forest it was down again into a valley, through which if we were correct with our navigation the road to Bolzano and the River Oglio should be running. We walked on the road for a short distance, but didn't feel safe as there was a lot of traffic, including German trucks, and we could see a town ahead of us. This was Capo di Ponte, proving our directions to be okay. We climbed up the side of the valley and found a track, which was running in the same direction as the road. The trail took us to a number of small villages which we skirted. After three or four detours we gave up and walked through the next few. Yet again we told the tale at an isolated farm and were given a meal and a blanket in a barn.

The next day, 11 October, we continued along the side of the valley, still running parallel to the road, and soon we were looking down on the sizeable town of Edolo. There were a lot of Germans to be seen. We were too far to the east so headed west over another road. It was here that we had our worst scare. We were walking along looking for a track when we were overtaken by a German staff car. Thirty yards or so past us the driver revved up his engine and changed gear. We thought that he was stopping for us but it turned out that he was preparing to cross a bridge and take the bend beyond. We got off the road and started climbing into the hills where we felt safe. As usual we were soon on our way down into a valley and again were given a meal and shelter at a farm.

Hugh asked the farmer and his son if they would guide us over the border into Switzerland but they refused. However, they told us that the frontier ran along the side of Mount Combolo, with part of the mountain in Italy and part in Switzerland. As far as they knew there were no fortifications. Hugh and I decided to start early the next day, get onto the mountain, which according to our map was about 3,000 metres, and find a hiding place. Once it was dark we would climb slowly to the top of the mountain and know that we would be in Switzerland.

On 12 October we set off at 4am, walked along the road past Tirano and on to Villa di Tirano at the foot of the mountain, arriving about 8am. We found a track leading upwards into the forest. We didn't go together. One of us hid and kept watch while the other went on another 50 or 60 yards, but this elaborate procedure soon proved unnecessary as we became enveloped in a thick mist.

We decided to go on up rather than wait for the night. We still moved as quietly as possible. About 2pm Hugh grabbed my arm. I immediately thought we had been spotted. But he pulled me back and over to his right and pointed to a concrete block. On the side we were on it said *Svizzera* and on the other, *Italia*. We searched to the left and right and found similar slabs. We started to walk into Switzerland, but with one accord and without a word to one another, we turned, walked back into Italy, joined hands and jumped over an imaginary line between two of the blocks. Childish and foolhardy but an expression of our joy at being free after nearly 30 months of captivity.

We went on into Switzerland, watching carefully in case we recrossed into Italy. We were not sure if it was safe to start going down rather than up. After a while we sat and rested for an hour. The track we were on was more level and tending downwards. The mist had risen and the sun was shining. We set off again, still keeping as quiet as possible. I think that it was about 4pm when we got another shock. A soldier stepped out of a perfect hide with a rifle pointed at us and a voice behind us said 'Halt!' It was another soldier covering us with a rifle. The guards' uniforms and helmets were different from German or Italian ones, so we were happy to put our hands up. Hugh said in Italian that we were escaped prisoners. The soldier in front spoke some English so we told him who we were. We were escorted down to barracks and greeted by the cook: 'Ah, two English boys, have some tea, yes!' We didn't advise him that we were a Rhodesian and a Scot.

The next day we were taken to Campocologno and then by train over the Bernina Pass to Samedan, where we were handed over to British soldiers operating in civilian clothing. We were put in a hotel, interrogated and watched by both the British and Swiss. After four days we were told that we had been authenticated.

We had a trip to St Moritz and were soon on our way to Wil, which was the HQ for the hundreds of prisoners who had escaped into Switzerland. The following day, with very little notice, Hugh and I were split up. He was going to join the RAF officers in Arosa and I was to leave for a small village, Schonengrund in Canton Appenzell, where about 100 British troops were billeted. It was sad to be separated. When we arrived at Wil we had to sign a declaration to the effect that we would not attempt to leave Switzerland without the permission of both the British and Swiss authorities. [2]

Allied servicemen remained in Switzerland for up to a year. From Wil they were sent to detachments in the neighbouring countryside and billeted in empty buildings such as factories and schools. Officers were provided with an allowance and obtained their own food and lodging.

Movement was restricted to the village boundary and the men had to be back in their dormitories by 10 o' clock at night, but they received pocket money and a monthly postage allowance and there was the chance of weekend leave. A hotel was also requisitioned at Adelboden and the servicemen were able to enjoy a month of winter sports.

In January 1944, the Swiss Government agreed that the *évadés* could volunteer for work. Those involved in forestry and land drainage were billeted in purpose-built barracks, while the ones engaged in agriculture lived with families on farms. The pay was two Swiss Francs a day and there was ten days extra leave every three months, with free rail travel and a ration allowance. Summer camps were eventually opened at Arosa and Caux and some of the smaller detachments were closed. However, all leave was cancelled after the Allied invasion of Normandy on 6 June.

The liberation of southern France by the Allied 7th Army in Operation Anvil/Dragoon in August opened up a land corridor and allowed the repatriation of the men by the end of the year. MI 9's Return of Escapers and Evaders up to 30 June 1945 reveals that there had been 5,143 Allied servicemen in Switzerland.

NOTES

[1] Of the remaining New Zealand servicemen who reached Switzerland, 20 per cent were from PG 107 Torviscosa and the final 10 per cent from various camps. The overall figures for New Zealand prisoners of war in Italy were: Number at the time of the Armistice: 3,700 approximately, escaped to Switzerland: 108, escaped to Allied lines: 339, killed at large: 7, killed in transit north: 8, fate unknown: 6, and transferred to Germany: 3,200 approximately.

[2] Information credit: The narrative is based on a manuscript kindly supplied by John Muir.

70

6 THE GILDED CAGE

In the spring of 1943, the twin castles of Montalbo and Rezzanello in my family's home province of Piacenza ceased to be camps for Commonwealth prisoners of war. This left only one gaol, but it was a very superior establishment.

In 1942, the Italian Government had requisitioned a former stately home to become the country's main camp for senior officers. The prison was designated PG 29 Veano, taking its name from a hamlet in the commune of Vigolzone consisting of just four houses, a small church and the Villa Alberoni, an impressive three-storey building. In the nineteenth century the villa was the residence of the Countess Bianchi-Costa. Afterwards it was owned by the Opera Pia Alberoni religious foundation and used as a training college for priests.

Veano is approached along a winding country road through rich farming country that links the Trebbia and Nure Valleys. The hamlet is in an elevated position, though only 20 kilometres from the city of Piacenza on the plain. On a clear day there is a lovely view of the Alps, over 100 kilometres away.

PG 29 opened on 1 May 1942. Soon tales began to circulate in the neighbourhood of spectacular escape attempts, of famous people held in the camp and of comfort and abundance in the middle of shortage and rationing. Farmer Chiesa recalled: 'The prisoners were far better off than their guards. The foreigners arrived thin and weak, but left fat and reinvigorated as if they had been on a cure.' The priest of Veano, Don Antonio Callegari, added: 'It was not the prison camp of popular imagination, but more like a comfortable hotel providing a pleasant stay.'

Two or three heavy lorries were required to carry up the Red Cross parcels each week and a wagon pulled by two mules would also arrive loaded with fresh produce from Salsomaggiore. The prisoners had butter, tinned foods, coffee, chocolate and sugar, and in addition they could buy chickens and eggs from the farmers with coupons supplied by the Commandant. To many of the Italians Veano became known as *la prigione dorata*, figuratively the gilded cage.

In a report made to the War Office, Admiral Sir Walter Cowan, DSO, who was repatriated in March 1943, wrote:

> One thing that astonished me was the way the days rather flew by, owing I think to there being no horizon, no

term of weeks or months to live down and count the days off. The life is rather that of a cow in the field, but every day full of hope and every now and then an abnormal wave of it ... About three times in the night every room would be visited by the guards and also three times each day at uncertain times we would all be fallen in and mustered. After every attempted escape there would be a most rigorous search of everyone and everything, which would take many hours. One understands it to be far harder to escape from Italy than from Germany. [1]

We have a snapshot of Veano only a week before the announcement of the Armistice in a report from the Georges Bonnant, Attaché to the Swiss Legation, Service of Foreign Interests, who made a visit of inspection on 1 September 1943.

There were 268 prisoners, made up of 206 officers and 62 'other ranks' who were volunteer orderlies. Two hundred and fifty four of the men were British, with the other 14 Australian, Canadian, Irish, Maltese, New Zealander, Polish and South African. Two hundred and fifty eight of the servicemen were from the Army, six were Air Force officers and four Navy 'other ranks.' The Senior British Officer was Colonel Younghusband and the Italian Commandant, Colonel Cornaggia Medici Castiglioni, from Milan. He had replaced the original Commandant, Colonel Poggiali, of Ravenna. The Italian garrison consisted of 150 soldiers and *Carabinieri*, the army corps that is also a police force.

The camp was intended for officers of field rank, majors and lieutenant colonels, but as the tide of war turned against the Allies in North Africa over the summer more junior captives also had to be accommodated. This led to constant complaints of overcrowding from the inmates. The neutral inspectors commented: 'The Italian General Staff do not appear to understand the situation for nothing has been done as a result of the numerous protests we have made during the last year.'

In addition, 28 officers had arrived from Hospital Camp 207, which had been bombed out of Milan. The senior officer, Australian Lieutenant Colonel Loris Cooper, reported that the hospital was only 500 yards from the railway station. The area had been subjected to eight aerial bombardments and the men forced to hide in a cellar. Finally, the building had been hit and the camp dissolved.

There were frequent escape attempts from PG 29, which the Italians put down to the wish to break the monotony of camp life and to the pleasure of witnessing the discomfort of the guards and their frantic efforts to round up the runaways.

Major Patrick Clayton created documents and maps for the escapers. He had been awarded the DSO for his part in forming the Long Range Desert Group and for raids on Italian outposts. In January 1941 he was wounded and captured. Before the war the major had explored and charted the deserts of Egypt and Libya. Among his companions was 'Count' Laszlo Almasy, the Hungarian adventurer and German spy whose character was fictionalised in Michael Ondaatje's 1992 book, *The English Patient*, and in the 1997 film of the same name which won nine Academy Awards.

One officer tried to leave Veano disguised as a building worker. Another hid inside a milk churn due for collection. Others attempted to escape from the barber's shop, through the cellar, and up the chimney of the library. A Captain Fraser was shot in the hand by an Italian sergeant while trying to break out of a kitchen used by the prisoners. However, only on a few occasions did escapers manage to leave the immediate vicinity of the camp.

The Nure Valley at Bettola. (Cordani)

The first success was that of Brigadier George Clifton, DSO, MC, commander of the New Zealand 6th Brigade in North Africa, who was nicknamed 'The Flying Kiwi.' In mid February 1943 he made what he later described as his 'high speed escape,' travelling the 90 kilometres to the Swiss border in just 20 hours. The brigadier took a carriage outside the railway station in Como and proceeded towards the Villa d' Este and the road for the mountains. He was arrested within yards of the frontier fence by two suspicious *Alpini*, the Italian mountain troops. After the usual punishment of 30 days in solitary confinement, George Clifton was sent to PG 5 Gavi, the 'bad boys' camp.' The Commandant at Veano, whom Sir Walter had described as 'a gentleman,' was replaced shortly afterwards. Brigadier Clifton made a total of nine escape attempts during his time as a prisoner of war, succeeding in gaining his freedom on the last. [2]

The largest breakout was through a tunnel. The courtyard at Veano was divided into two areas, one given over to games of volleyball and the other to an orchard where the prisoners established a kitchen garden. But as well as potatoes and tomatoes a team of officers led by Brigadier Clifton's compatriot, Major Hilary Evans, cultivated schemes of escape. For three months they excavated a passageway from the garden to an area outside the camp's double tier of barbed wire fencing. The tunnel was 14 metres long, 5 metres deep and half a metre wide. It was shored up by planking salvaged from Red Cross containers.

During a film show at the camp, Major Evans led 14 prisoners through the tunnel. However, most of the escapers were soon rounded up and returned to the camp. The major was free the longest. He was arrested by two *Carabinieri* on bicycles north of Rome after two weeks. The recapture created added disappointment at Veano as many inmates had placed bets with their bookmaker on Major Evans retaining his liberty.

In another attempt, Major Harold Jan Branson from the Royal Artillery was recaptured at Plaisance on 2 July 1943. On his return, he was berated in front of all the officers by General Messina, the new commandant of the zone embracing the camp. The apologetic interpreter translated his comments as: 'Major Branson, the general is sorry you have come back with your face not smashed in.'

As the summer progressed, the prisoners became increasingly unruly. Whenever a British or American aircraft passed overhead the men ran to the windows, shouting loudly and waving sheets, forcing the guards to intervene to restore order.

On 1 September, Georges Bonnant reported that contrary to the practice in other camps, his team had not been allowed to talk freely and without witnesses to the SBO and other prisoners. In addition, 'relations between the authorities and the prisoners have been more strained since the change of the commandant of the zone.' [3]

News of the Armistice arrived at Veano exactly a week later, on the evening of 8 September. But it took almost two days for its effects to be fully felt.

In the meantime, in the words of one of the orderlies, Rifleman John Micallef: 'The Italian *Comandante* and our senior officer agreed what to do in the event that the Germans sought to transport us to Germany.'

On Thursday, 9 September, Colonel George Younghusband, the SBO, read out the 'stand fast order,' but reserve rations were issued and the prisoners were told to pack and be ready to leave at a moment's notice. An 80-foot section of the wire was cut and the men were allowed to wander in the neighbourhood of the camp.

News arrived that Germans were fighting Italians in Piacenza and soon defeated Italian troops began to arrive at the camp. That night over two thirds of the guards deserted.

On Friday morning, 10 September, Colonel Younghusband announced that Colonel Medici Castiglioni had told him that he no longer had enough troops to be able to guarantee the safety of the prisoners in the event of a German attack. The SBO informed his men that they were now free to leave, though he would remain in camp and recommended others to do so.

The Camp Commandant obtained supplies of currency and between 200 to 400 lire was issued to each man. The Italian advised the prisoners to disperse in the hills. After an early lunch the exodus began. It was 12.30 and the enemy was only four miles away. The alarm was sounded minutes later. The Germans fired random shots into the surrounding woods, looted the buildings, and failed to capture a single prisoner. The official record simply notes: 'On 10 September 1943, information was received the Germans were approaching the camp and the whole camp scattered into the countryside.' [4]

The chaplain to the Italian garrison at Veano for the three months up to the Armistice was Don Lorenzo Losini. He had completed his studies there when it was a seminary. Thanks to the Piacenza branch of the national partisan organisation, ANPI, I was in contact with Don Losini 60 years later. He graciously provided details of a diary he kept during that heady September. At the time the priest was aged 30. He had a smattering of English and soon got to know the prisoners, many of whom were eager to fraternise with the Italians.

The radio announcement of the Armistice was, Don Losini recalled, greeted with 'great joy' throughout Prison Camp No. 29, 'but at the same time with fear of attack by the Germans.' The diary for the next five days reads:

9 September - Mass of Thanks by the British Catholic chaplain. The Catholic prisoners and all the soldiers from the garrison attended, together with Colonel Cornaggia Medici, several locals and myself.

Around 11 o' clock the Commandant became perplexed. He had received no further orders and did not know what to do with the prisoners. The colonel consulted everyone. I told him: 'Set them free!' In fact after a while he opened up the camp and liberated all the prisoners. They rushed outside and flooded into the surrounding houses. The soldiers brought presents for everybody. They also came to our home, leaping over the wall of the pigeon coop. Piera called them inside. The musician from the camp who played the accordion began a performance. The instrument had been given as a present by the Papal Nuncio on behalf of the Pope. Much wine was drunk.

Two prisoners gave my sisters overcoats, sunglasses and bars of chocolate. Then two majors also arrived. They offered my father lots of tobacco and gave me a book from their library, which was entitled *The Hill of the Doves*.

In the evening, our first fears. We heard of German anger and threats of reprisals against 'the traitors.'

During the night seven soldiers and three Air Force captains lodged under our portico. In the morning we also made coffee for them. They repaid us with packets of tea.

Together with the Catholic chaplain, Colonel Fischel, I visited the priest of Veano, Don Antonio Callegari, at around five in the evening. A drinks party!

A detachment from the 1st Heavy Regiment arrived at the camp, commanded by Major Gioffrè. He was ordered by the camp commandant to defend the prisoners against the Germans or to let them go free. The soldiers placed a machine gun facing Ancarano. In fact, the Germans arrived from Bobbio, but by then the camp was already empty.

10 September - I went to Rivergaro but soon returned. I found our house full of Englishmen. They were very worried. At midday I went out to see what was going on. When I returned my family were already at table with several of the men. Suddenly other frightened Englishmen arrived, saying: 'The Germans! The Germans!' We gave them bread and salami and made them flee.

Fortunately, it was a false alarm ... but at five in the evening the Germans really arrived, coming from Bobbio, firstly two soldiers on a motorbike and, shortly afterwards, a jeep with an officer and several troops. I was at the camp and tried to be friendly towards them.

Imprudently, I asked: 'Where are you from?' One replied in Latin: '*Non possum dicere,*' I cannot say.

However, another answered me: 'From Bobbio.' The interpreter, Lieutenant Denti, and the doctor, Captain Bonometti, were taken prisoner. Frightened, I made for home and had a bad night. We heard frequent musket fire.

11 September - Many German lorries arrived and the troops spent the next days and nights plundering the camp. Also, several armoured cars came to act as garrison.

My sister, Ines, went with the fiancée of Lieutenant Denti to visit him at the camp. They passed him a rucksack and a parcel through a window. But they were seen by a German who pointed a pistol at them, greatly frightening the young ladies.

12 September - I went to the church to celebrate mass and saw five armoured cars. There was great movement in the camp.

Late in the evening, the two Englishmen who had eaten with us returned to our home. One was wounded. There was a lot of commotion. We embraced them. They wanted to give themselves up to the Germans, but we dissuaded them and provided refreshment. Three days later we saw the soldiers again, at the bottom of our land, and they seemed happy. We gave them bread, salami and tobacco.

13 September - After emptying the camp most of the Germans went away. They left a small garrison of a sergeant and five troops in an outside barracks. We heard that they were selling items from the camp. Perhaps they had hidden them. Summoning my courage, I took them a white loaf and a bottle of wine. They shook my hand and gave me a fine pair of English shoes. The following evening two of the Germans came to our house. They sat outside and played a mouth organ. We called them in to eat grapes. They repaid us with a nice English overcoat. After several days these particular soldiers left.

A German saw me outside the camp and sold me another pair of English shoes for 100 lire.

Later the camp was equipped to accommodate members of the *Todt* organisation working on the airdrome at San Damiano.

Don Losini's diary ends with this entry:

1 October - Friday. British reconnaissance aircraft bombed the airfield at San Damiano. Much anti-aircraft fire. A rain of splinters fell around us too.

In the days and months that followed, many British prisoners who had not been able to escape hid in farmhouses and woods, aided by the local countryfolk. I was also often to be found taking goods to prisoners in hiding. But to avoid arousing the suspicion of the occasional German or Fascist who sometimes carried out a check, I always took my cassock and stole with me, as if I was making a visit to a sick parishioner.

The escapers faced four main choices. They could remain in the area until circumstances became clearer, move north towards Switzerland, south to friendly forces, or west to the coast where Allied landings were rumoured. In practice, most escapers from Veano remained in the vicinity of the camp for about a fortnight and then began to disperse. The priest of Veano, Don Callegari,

78

sheltered a colonel for several days who was suffering with sciatica. He was then taken to the mountains by ox cart. Veano might only be 20 kilometres from the city of Piacenza, with half of that along the plain, but in the opposite direction there is the high country, with ridges, thick beech woods and the most secluded area in the province.

Several officers from PG 29 became famous partisans. Major d' Arcy Mander made his way to Rome and created his own intelligence network. Major Gordon Lett walked to the Rossano Valley in northern Tuscany and formed his International Battalion. Also on the Fifth Army front, Major AJ (Tony) Oldham led the Lunese Division of 3,500 men. Two escapers from Veano even became noted partisans in the Nure Valley itself, as we shall see in the next chapter.

Among the senior officers who reached Switzerland were lieutenant colonels Bush and Cooper from the Green Howards, Norman from the East Yorkshire Regiment (the first SBO at PG 49 Fontanellato), and Foote and Reynolds from the Royal Tank Regiment.

Typical upland village in the Province of Piacenza: Groppo Ducale, Bettola. (Cordani)

They were helped by an escape line created by Lieutenant Colonel N Boddington of the Royal Engineers. From a safe house in the mountains he located fellow servicemen and fed them along a network that was accurately christened by Major Mander a 'guide line.' For three weeks the lieutenant colonel was assisted by tank Brigade Major AHG (Tony) Dobson until he too decided to attempt an escape. The Italian side of the organisation was handled by a garage owner who hired cars to the Germans. His secret activities were eventually discovered and he was shot.

Tony Dobson paired off with another major from the camp called Stephen Radcliffe. They were provided with a new suit, a shirt, tie and hat each, and set off at the end of October. The officers were taken to Piacenza station and travelled onto Milan. They were escorted by two middle aged partisan wireless operators who were going to the British Embassy in Bern to obtain new code sheets.

In the city the group walked from the *Stazione Centrale* to *Milano Nord* where they caught a train for the 46-kilometre journey to Como. Passing the military headquarters, the escapers boarded the ferry along the lake. The boat was full of schoolgirls on an outing. The men disembarked at the resort of Menaggio and climbed a steep track to the home of their guide for the last leg of the journey. He was an Italian *Bersagliere* soldier and frontier guard. For 50 lire a time he was willing to help fugitives across the border. However, the infantryman said it was too dangerous for them to stay the night with him and the men were forced to undertake a 2,000-foot climb to his uncle's chalet.

The escapers set off before dawn next day. It began to snow and when they reached the border they found it was marked by a ten-foot high chain link fence topped by barbed wire. The *Bersagliere* simply lifted a section of the fence and the men scrambled underneath. The guard threw them their belongings, presented arms and waved farewell.

Within weeks the Fascists began to intercept servicemen and their helpers and a less direct route via Turin had to be used by the escape line.

* * *

One of the officers who decided to stay near the camp in the hope of Allied landings in the north was Major Dennis Whitehead of the Green Howards. Before the war he had been an estate agent and territorial. At Veano the officer shared a room with Major d' Arcy Mander, from the same regiment.

Major Whitehead left the camp with four members of the East Yorkshire Regiment. They lived in the woods on Red Cross supplies brought from the camp and threw blankets over their shoulders for warmth. When it was found the locals were not only friendly but eager to help, the officers descended to a different farm each night, sleeping in the barn and leaving in the morning with a chunk of bread and maybe some cheese or fruit. They abandoned their battledress for civilian garments, once even swapping clothes with a scarecrow.

The quintet of soldiers eventually split up to reduce the burden on any one host. The major teamed up with Captain DE Field of the East Yorkshire Regiment.

Conditions deteriorated with the onset of winter and the two friends decided to strike out for Switzerland. They were helped in their decision by a message from Lieutenant Colonel Foote. He told them that the 'guide line' was a success and that he and several other officers were already safely in the Confederation. In addition, they were not being held in camps, enjoyed a measure of freedom and had the opportunity to plan a final escape through France and Spain.

The pair set off at first light on Monday, 22 November. They were surprised to find seven fellow officers from Veano already waiting at the rendezvous. The men were about to leave for Piacenza station to catch a train for Turin, a journey of 188 kilometres, nowadays taking little over two hours. One of the group, Major LS Bailey, RASC, was six foot three inches tall and the guide said that he would attract attention. It would be better for him to join Field and Whitehead in their attempt, which would be by night.

The three officers left on the Thursday, three days later, with a young woman as their guide. The plan was to catch the workman's train for Turin at Piacenza, lie up during the day and move towards the border the following night. However, the escapers had only reached the long bridge at Bettola when they ran into a patrol of Fascist militia led by a ruthless officer, Lieutenant Zanoni. Major Bailey and Major Whitehead were stopped and arrested as the lieutenant suspected they were Italians dodging the call up. Captain Field and the guide passed unchallenged. But when Zanoni discovered that his two captives were actually escaped British officers it suddenly dawned on him that the two others must also have been part of the group. The Fascists raced to the station and hauled Captain Field and the guide off the train. In further searches the militia discovered four more prisoners of war.

Meanwhile, majors Bailey and Whitehead were imprisoned in the town hall at Bettola. They were put in an office and held at gunpoint. However, when the guard placed his pistol on the desk while he searched their possessions the officers were able to knock him to the floor, recover their belongings, vandalise the office and flee into the night. The escapers retraced their footsteps and were soon back with their peasant helpers. Lieutenant Zanoni falsely claimed that the officers had murdered the guard and a large reward was posted for their recapture.

The two friends lay low until after Christmas 1943, but at the end of January renewed their efforts to escape. This time they contacted the local black market boss, a young man with his own lorry and a travel pass from the Germans which allowed him to travel freely around the countryside. The majors teamed up with a South African escaper and they hid among wine barrels on the back of the lorry. But instead of driving them to meet their guide, the crook took them straight to a yard full of rifle-wielding militia led by Lieutenant Zanoni. He stood the officers against a wall and said he was going to shoot them, but changed his mind at the last minute. Dennis Whitehead recalled these events in a letter sent after the war from Bridlington to one of his main Italian helpers, Maria Carella Baio:

> Captain Field, Major Bailey and I were captured in Bettola by Zanoni, as you've already heard. He stopped us to ask for our papers as we appeared to be of military age and should have reported to the barracks in Piacenza that very day.
>
> Captain Field did not manage to escape and was taken to Germany, but we had another two months in the mountains before we again tried to get through to Switzerland.
>
> Later, we were betrayed into the hands of Zanoni, together with Sergeant Major Brown, the South African, through the treachery of our guide, Pietro from Russi, and another older man whose name I cannot recall for certain, but which was something like Masini. I remember him well.
>
> It was only after we had been in Germany for some time that we were able to convince ourselves that Pietro, whose

family had been so kind to us over the whole period we were in the mountains, had betrayed us. I hear that he is serving 12 years in prison as a collaborator. Masini has not yet been traced, but I have a letter from the War Crimes Department telling me that Zanoni was sentenced to death and executed last year ... which saved us a certain amount of trouble.

Luckily for us, Zanoni did not have the courage to shoot us out of hand as he would have wished, but instead took us to the Garibaldi Barracks and handed us over without any papers as British spies in civilian clothing. Sergeant Major Brown was held separately from us.

We were pushed into the Condemned Cell to be shot on the Monday morning when the Commandant returned. Unfortunately for him, it was only Friday evening. By Saturday I had convinced the Officer in Charge that I was a British officer. On Sunday a British colonel whom I knew very well [Arthur Robinson, an anti-aircraft gunnery officer who had also been at Veano] was brought into the prison. We were not allowed to contact others in the cells, but by shouting through the walls we told him we were being held as spies. When the Germans came to fetch him on Monday, he told them he could give the names of two other British officers now held. The Germans at once ordered an inspection of the prison and we were discovered.

Later we went on to Germany and met again Captain Field and others who had been captured.

I remember Francesco telling me that he had been taken to your flat and at once police had appeared and arrested him and his friends, also you and your husband and son. I would be interested to hear the outcome of your story.

Fortunately, Signora Baio provided the sequel in a book about her wartime experiences entitled *Le Vere Origini della Resistenza Piacentina,* The True Origins of the Piacentine Resistance, which was published in 1976. In a commentary on the work, Maria Luisa Cerri wrote: 'It reveals the risks and the personal sacrifices endured by the authoress and her family owing to their main activity of helping British ex prisoners.' This is the topic of the next chapter.

NOTES

[1] TNA: PRO WO 224/112 *Description of Camp 29 written by Admiral Sir Walter Cowan, who left there on 6 March 1943.*
The admiral began his service career as early as 1884 and served in all the major conflicts of the British Empire. At age 68 on the outbreak of the Second World War he petitioned the Admiralty for an appointment. Sir Walter served as liaison officer with the commandos and was captured at Bir Hakeim in Libya in 1942. On his return from Italy he was awarded the Bar to the DSO he had won over 40 years earlier in the Sudan. In 1944 the admiral was back in Italy with the Second Commando Brigade.
[2] See *The Happy Hunted* by Brigadier George Clifton, DSO, MC.
[3] TNA: PRO WO 224/112 *Report No. 7 on Camp No. 29 for British prisoners of war in Italian hands.*
[4] TNA: PRO WO 224/179.

7 THE RED STAR

The new Fascist Republic made giving aid and comfort to enemy prisoners of war a treasonable offence in October 1943. The penalty could be capital punishment. Still, as we have already seen, Allied servicemen received spontaneous assistance across occupied Italy.

The civilians had a secret weapon, the ties of family and friendship which made it hard for the authorities to penetrate their activities. But although difficult it was not impossible. There were many spies and informers.

Maria Carella Baio's husband, Francesco, was a shopkeeper in the centre of Piacenza. They had an apartment nearby, as well as a home in Bettola, main town of the valley. It soon became a rebel staging post between the city and the mountains. Cesare Baio, the son, was a student and partisan.

Major Whitehead first met Francesco and Cesare shortly after his escape from PG 29 Veano. It was in the mountains at Nicelli at the home of Doro Lanza, a lawyer and the first partisan commander. Together with a Signor Silvio Nuvoloni the pair were acting as guides to a group of South Africans who had jumped from a prison train near Piacenza. They included a black soldier called Francis, in Italian *Francesco*.

Signora Baio related that the South Africans had been brought to her house in Bettola by Emilio Canzi, later partisan leader of the province. It was 27 September 1943, the last Monday in the month, the day of a traditional market. Signora Baio offered to escort one of the prisoners out of the town centre. Reginald was tall and used to marching. The more the lady speeded up to separate herself from him, the more closely he followed her. Even so, they reached the outskirts safely, passing under the noses of a notorious *Carabiniere* sergeant and Fascist troops.

At the time, the priest of San Giovanni, Don Maiocchi, was sheltering escaped prisoners in his rectory. They included Colonel Fencior of the Guards and the Australian Lieutenant Colonel Loris Cooper. He also spent three days at the Baio apartment in Piacenza. When it became too dangerous for the soldiers to remain they were escorted to the mountains and entrusted to the priest at Pellacini di Cogno San Bassano, where there was already a nucleus of foreign prisoners. As mentioned in the last chapter, Loris Cooper was among the senior officers who eventually escaped along the 'guide line' to Switzerland.

The escapers most reluctant to follow advice were Sikhs. Among other things they refused to cut their hair and stayed together in a group. At Borgotrebbia four of the Indians concealed themselves in a haystack during a Fascist raid. They were in so deep that not even bayonets thrust into the hay could force them out. Some sustained wounds but bore the pain in silence. The Fascists concluded they had chosen the wrong target and withdrew. The people rushed to help the wounded men and eventually they were taken to safety in the mountains.

Signora Baio recalled the help given by the Resistance to Allied escapers:

> The first leaders of the partisan bands began to appear, among them 'il Moro' (Livio Sormani). At Montechiaro di Bettola he assisted large groups of prisoners of varying nationalities. Thanks to the willing cooperation of the local people he provided assistance of every kind. Oblivious to the danger he ran, Sormani frequented the Piacentine inns on market days, asking friends and acquaintances for donations of money and in kind 'for the lads.' And as everyone understood his coded message they gave as much as they could.
>
> Several merchants who had been evacuated from Piacenza provided articles of clothing: Signor Ronchini gave hats, Signori Grilli and Cavallari furnished ties, and others donated sets of everyday garments.
>
> Eventually spies discovered the refuge that was increasingly involved with these activities. A number of prisoners were captured when preparations were being made for their escape and several local people were rounded up as traitors to the regime. I was one of them. But through luck and guile Sormani managed to evade the trap. [1]

On Saturday, 8 January 1944, the Fascist newspaper, *La Scure*, (The Axe), reported the arrests:

> The Special Branch of the National Republican Guard (GNR) continues its steadfast work in smashing every criminal activity that endangers the State. After diligent enquiries the legionaries learned that several enemy prisoners were being sheltered at 41, Via Cavour, Piacenza,

the home of Francesco Baio, aged 50, a shopkeeper with a varnish shop at 34, Via Cittadella. The other evening the militia broke into the Baio household and arrested three foreigners who were later identified as South African prisoners of war. They were taken into custody, together with their hosts, Francesco Baio, his wife Maria Carella Baio, aged 46, and their son Cesare Baio, aged 20, who will appear before the Military Tribunal of War.

The following day the newspaper had another scoop:

We had only just reported that the GNR had arrested three prisoners from the British Army together with those harbouring them when further information was received that makes the position of the Baio family even worse.

Yesterday three British prisoners of war were taken by surprise outside the house and arrested by the militia while waiting to receive hospitality. The captives were evidently ignorant of the fact that the refuge had been discovered and their collaborators sent to gaol. Fortunately, these circumstances allowed the prisoners to be rounded up as well and places the Baio case on the level of criminal complicity with the enemy.

Signora Baio was sentenced to eight months imprisonment and her husband and son to deportation to a concentration camp in Germany. They worked in a factory as part of a forced labour detachment. Owing to the conditions Cesare fell ill and required medical treatment. While visiting the doctor there was an air raid and both the young Italian and his guard were killed by Allied bombs. It was 14 October 1944.

In a letter to Signora Baio sent just after the war, Lieutenant Colonel Loris Cooper, then serving with the 13th Battalion, The Sherwood Foresters, wrote:

Naturally I remember you all very well and how kind and friendly you were to me. I was very sad to hear what had happened to you. I already had the feeling that you had many problems. I remember Masini and hope he has been punished for the cruel deed he did you. I am with you, Dear Lady, in the grief for the loss of your dear son.

He was a fine boy and died too young. My words are not able to fully express my thoughts. I hope that your husband is with you once more and that you are again in your home.

I also hope that the Allied Commission has recognised your sacrifices and is working on your behalf. I gave your name to our War Office when I arrived in England. I was in France for some time with the Americans, then six weeks in England and one in Burma. Now I am in India and as soon as I am able I shall come to see you and thank you. You were all so marvellous towards us and the consequences you suffered were so harsh.

After serving her term of imprisonment, Signora Baio resumed her mission to help foreign prisoners and local partisans with even greater vigour.

In her absence, the armed Resistance in the Nure Valley had been transformed. In March 1944, the provincial Liberation Committee brought an escaped Yugoslav officer from Bardi to unite four small bands in the Bettola area. Dusan Milic, known as Montenegrino, was judged to be 'experienced in command and in guerrilla warfare.' The new detachment was christened the *Stella Rossa*, or Red Star.

Plaque commemorating the award of a Silver Medal to Bettola in 1994 in recognition of its wartime role as the centre of Resistance in Piacenza. (Cordani)

88

It seems that during a skirmish with the enemy the partisans from various small groups had stuck a red cloth on their jackets to identify themselves to one another. The priest of Cassano had suggested The Scarlet Pimpernel as a suitable name for the new unit, but perhaps wisely, Red Star was chosen instead, not least for its political significance. Of all the partisan formations in the province the Garibaldi brigades from the Nure Valley were the only ones to which the label Communist could even be loosely applied. Their men gave the clenched fist salute and wore the red star on their uniforms.

The *Stella Rossa* moved into the mountains and by the end of May had grown to three battalions. One was led by Gian Maria Molinari, known as Gianmaria, and the other two by British officers, both escaped prisoners of war from Veano. Captain Archibald Donald Mackenzie of the 2nd Battalion, Queen's Own Cameron Highlanders, was from Kincardineshire in Scotland. Captain (later Colonel) Tresham Gregg of the Royal Tank Regiment was an Irishman. To the Italians the officers were simply known by their *nomi di battaglia*, Mak and Ganna. In late June, the formation was granted recognition as a brigade, the *60th Brigata d'Assalto Garibaldi 'Stella Rossa.'* Captain Mackenzie became its *Capo di Stato Maggiore* (CSM), or Chief of Staff.

Maria Carella Baio was introduced to the captains by her nephew, Franco Pareti, an artillery lieutenant who had chosen the road of anti-Fascism after 8 September. He first met the pair among a group of seven escapers in the mountains at Cassimoreno. 'The others were elderly colonels,' Signora Baio recalled. She added, 'Mak' and 'Ganna' remained among us the longest, sharing the risks and discomforts of the armed struggle. I knew 'Ganna' from my sister's bar. 'Mak' often came to my home and admired the view of Bettola from the window, saying: 'A strategic location.'

In a report in December, Captain Tresham Gregg related that the 60th Brigade had 800 well-armed men, equipped with a mortar, four bazookas, grenade launchers, machine guns and rifles. They also had about 40 vehicles. He added:

> Commander 'Montenegrino,' Dusan Milic, Reserve Lieutenant in the Yugoslav Army, was a capable and brave leader when we were fighting in the mountains, but after we had captured Bettola in July 1944 he thought only of women and enjoying himself ...

The brigade is more interested in fighting than talking about politics. More than any other brigade it has been commanded by Britishers.

Until October 1944 the brigade was engaged in clearing the enemy out of the Nure Valley and in capturing the towns of Ferriere, Bettola and Pontedellolio. After the capture of this last town the brigade was able to operate on the plain and finally on the Via Emilia east of Piacenza. Morale is good, the 60th Brigade has the best fighting spirit of any in this province. [2]

There was another partisan brigade higher in the valley, the *59th Brigata Garibaldina 'Caio,'* led by a naval officer, Ernesto Poldrugo, who was known as Istriano. In August the formation decided to move over the mountains to Liguria owing to disagreements with 'Montenegrino.' The following month the 60th Brigade ceded liberated territory on the left bank of the Nure to a new *61st Brigata d'Assalto Garibaldi 'Valnure'* and occupied the whole upper valley left free by the 59th Brigade.

The central command for the province, the *Comando Unico*, was also based at Bettola. It was led by Emilio Canzi (Ezio Franchi), veteran of the Spanish Civil War and anti-Fascist activist since 1922. He had been chosen by the partisan leaders. One of his former commandants told me: 'We only knew about blowing up trains. He was experienced in politics.' Captain Gregg judged Canzi to be 'lacking in the higher qualities of an organiser,' but added, 'this deficiency was not greatly felt as he is surrounded by several men capable in this respect.' Anyway, he was 'very pro-British and American and is a man to whom it will pay to give all possible support.'

Commandant Canzi was abruptly sacked by the regional military command in April 1945. It was a Communist coup with the support of the British No. 1 Special Force Mission of Major Stephen Hastings, as recounted in my book, *Escape from Italy, 1943-45.* [3]

Emilio Canzi's Chief of Staff was 'Bandiera,' a lawyer and *Alpini* officer whose real name was Leonida Patrignani. He was head of No. 1 Special Force mission *La Quercia*, also known as *Conte*, and had entered Italy through Switzerland with instructions to organise sabotage work on the Via Emilia. Very early on the officer lost his wireless telegraphy (W/T) set and

90

joined Captain Cossu of the *Giustizia e Libertà* Division as *Capo di Stato Maggiore.*

The military intelligence section was run by an Italian known as Dedalo, who collated information from many sources. Among the people secretly working for him were the Chief of Staff of the Fascist *Littorio* Division and an employee of the Political Office in Piacenza.

The partisans deployed a team of spies, mostly women, under the leadership of Antonio Bosi of Riva and a Jewish engineer from Piacenza called Nicola Cantù. The agents returned with information on the divisional signs, weapons and equipment of all Fascist and German troops in the area.

The intelligence reports compiled by 'Dedalo' were sent on to an OSS mission codenamed Liviere. Some information was also forwarded to Major Gordon Lett's Blundell Mission in northern Tuscany and to another American mission. It was known as Roberto after its leader, a capable Italian parachute lieutenant. He formed a squad of 15 men that included Gunner Ronald Riches, a Londoner in the Royal Artillery. The Italian visited Captain Gregg in October and said that he had received orders to operate in his area. He was sent to Bore and provided with a house, car, rations and every assistance in obtaining information by the partisan commander *'Giovanni lo Slavo.'* In the middle of November, the OSS agent also requested that drop zones for the reception of weapons and supplies be organised. Two large supply operations were carried out by daylight.

Relations with another mission were not so clear cut. In September, the captain carried out written orders from the Liberation Committee in Milan to arrest a young Italian known as Oliviere. He had settled at Gropparello with two other men. They claimed to be Allied agents, but none of the messages identifying aerial targets given them for transmission by W/T ever seemed to result in bombing raids. When the leader of the group turned up at Bettola to remonstrate with Captain Gregg he signalled Allied HQ for instructions. The reply signed Macintosh - Major Charles Macintosh of No. 1 Special Force - said that 'Oliviere' was an Allied agent working for *Comando Unico* in Bettola and he was immediately released.

There was a clandestine radio station based at Bramaiano, near Bettola, which broadcast bulletins and propaganda twice a day. Four partisan newspapers were printed in the area, as well as many leaflets that were effective in inducing desertions.

A telephone exchange at Morfasso allowed communication between the Garibaldi brigades and *Comando Unico* in Bettola. There was also a W/T link between the headquarters and commanders on the right and left wings, *'Giovanni lo Slavo'* at Pellizone and 'Fausto' at Pecorara.

During the year to November 1944, the partisans took prisoner 312 Germans and about the same number of Fascists, excluding *Alpini*. The mountain troops were all conscripted during roundups and were a good source of recruits and supplies for the partisans. The prisoners were held in three camps, at Groppo Ducale, Farini D'Olmo and Ferriere. The men were well fed, and everything considered, humanely treated, with their main use as hostages and for exchange.

Tresham Gregg concluded that 'one of the main causes for the rapid development and good organisation of the partisan movement in the province of Piacenza was due to the good work that the *Comando Unico* did in instilling mutual confidence and a sense of cooperation between the different brigades. This was very important as generally there is considerable intrigue and jealousy between the heads of the various formations.'

There were four partisan commanders in addition to Dusan Milic, 'Montenegrino,' of the 60th Brigade. The second formation in the Nure Valley, the 61st Brigade, was led by Giuseppe Panni, an army officer known as Pippo. Another regular soldier, artillery lieutenant Giuseppe Prati, headed the *38th Brigata Garibaldi 'Wladimiro Bersani,'* based in the Arda Valley. Jovan Grkavac, *'Giovanni lo Slavo,'* like Milic a Yugoslav escaped prisoner of war, commanded the *62nd Brigata Garibaldi 'Luigi Evangelista,'* located on the border with Parma. Finally, Fausto Cossu, originally a *Carabiniere* lieutenant, led the *Divisione Giustizia e Libertà*, which covered all of the province west of the Trebbia River.

* * *

The advance of the partisans down the Nure Valley culminated in the taking of the town of Pontedellolio, which is only 23 kilometres from the city of Piacenza. The action began on Sunday, 1 October, when detachments from both brigades opened fire on Fascists in the school and garrison. Road and rail links were cut to impede reinforcements. Conditions were poor, with constant rain, mud underfoot and a mist. The enemy managed to break the blockade with an armoured car. It soon retreated under heavy fire, but returned early on Tuesday morning. On Wednesday night, 22 partisans infiltrated the town. In the morning, after a short but furious exchange of fire the Fascists requested terms. Captain Mackenzie stepped forward to negotiate the surrender. In the evening, 64 Fascist soldiers were marched off to imprisonment at Bettola and the insurgents helped themselves to large quantities of arms and ammunition.

On Friday morning, the Fascists launched a reprisal attack along the main road from Piacenza, which culminated in the sacking of civilian houses in Pontedellolio. However, by three in the afternoon the enemy force was in retreat and the partisans returned to re-establish order and to put out the fires. Three partisans who had tried to halt the advance of the column at Albarola were killed by fire from an armoured car: Carini, Merli and Captain Mackenzie, aged 29. He was loved by his men. The officer was buried with full military honours at Bettola in a moving ceremony attended by hundreds of partisans from across the valley and beyond.

Captain Gregg came to stay with Maria Carella Baio after the combat. He devoted much of his time to the rescue of his fellow soldiers, as the Signora recalled:

> One day an aircraft landed in the Morfasso area. A Sardinian captain with curly hair arrived at my house together with his men. They stayed several days. They were on a mission to carry secret orders to 'Ganna.' From then on all the British prisoners scattered across the mountains converged on my house to make arrangements with the captain for their journey through the Gothic Line and on to Allied Forces. [4]

In his report, Captain Gregg revealed that he was cooperating with the escape and evasion agency:

> 'Vermouth,' an A Force Mission, consisted of Lieutenant V Lockett, RA, Lieutenant Giovanni (Italian), Sergeant B Fick, UDF, and wireless operator Grassi. I worked in very close touch with this mission in that I used to send out partisan patrols to contact British and American escaped POWs or pilots. About 70 were collected at Bettola, where they were fed and accommodated at the expense of the *Comando Unico* and then given transport on to Bardi. All

the other members of the mission were very hard working and since September 1944 have sent through the line over 130 ex POWs and pilots.

At the beginning of October the radio of the Blundell mission of Major Gordon Lett was placed at the captain's disposal. As we saw in Chapter Three, the apparatus was based at Albareto, near Borgo Val di Taro, and operated by two agents codenamed Alfonso and Bianchi. To use the radio involved a substantial car ride for Tresham Gregg, followed by a seven-hour walk.

At some stage he met Lieutenant Commander Adrian Gallegos, RNVR, who was returning from 13 months behind enemy lines as a prisoner and escaper in Germany, Austria and Italy. The lieutenant commander carried news of the captain's activities back to Special Force HQ when he crossed the lines shortly afterwards. He reported:

> Gregg has no W/T set and came over to our area to send a signal requesting supplies. He asked me to give information to whomsoever might be interested. Briefly it is this: his area is very large and very rich - food, above all, is to be found in abundance. There are 10,000 partisans, 8,000 of whom are armed. He assured me that they were all very good men. The area includes many roads under partisan control and, in fact, he motored 70 kilometres before setting off on foot to reach us. The partisans are in control of oil wells producing 3,500 litres per day, of a wireless broadcasting station, of a newspaper, of a large model hospital and over 100 lorries and cars.
>
> The Germans don't seem to bother them much, but I expect that the bother will start when the front line gets nearer to their area. [5]

Tresham Gregg recalled:

> On my return journey along the Apennines after I had passed Bardi the conditions of the partisans and the civilians was becoming desperate because of Germans burning the villages, carrying away the cattle and murdering or deporting the civilian population.
>
> The people in the mountains are almost one hundred per cent anti-Fascist and pro-Ally. They do everything in their

94

power to help escaped British or American POWs. Lieutenant Franco Pareti of Bettola himself guided 42 ex POWs across the Po Valley, past Milan and on to Switzerland.

On 8 October 1944, Captain Gregg gave Maria Carella Baio this testimonial:

> The Baio family of Bettola have at considerable sacrifice helped British prisoners of war. They have helped them with shelter, food and information. Above all they have worked in our organisation for carrying POWs to Switzerland. In all, this organisation carried over 80 POWs to freedom, before a spy handed them over to the Germans. The family was then imprisoned. The mother was in prison for eight months, and the father and son were then taken to Germany, where they are still. I ask all officers and men of the Allied Armed Forces to help the family as much as possible.

The family was awarded an 'Alexander Certificate' at the end of the war, 'as a token of gratitude for and appreciation of the help given to the Soldiers, Sailors and Airmen of the British Commonwealth of Nations, which enabled them to escape from, or evade capture by the enemy.'

Captain Tresham Gregg left the Nure Valley on Wednesday, 29 November. He went on foot along the Apennines and crossed the front line at Monte Altissimo on Wednesday, 6 December.

His report was written eight days later. It concludes:

> While the partisan movement in the Apennines assumed very large proportions during the summer, I believe that in the coming winter it will very nearly die out of existence. The reasons for this are:
>
> a) The lack of munitions, food, supplies and clothing needed to last a winter in the mountains.
> b) The very large-scale operations which the Germans are carrying out and planning against areas held by the partisans.
> c) The lowering of morale due to the apparently immobile state of the front line in Italy. On three

occasions they have been told by the British radio to rise and smite the Hun as the day of liberation was at hand. On each occasion they attacked but found themselves no nearer liberation.

The partisans, I think, will split up into small bands of about 30 to 50 men.

The *Stella Rossa*, the *Valnure* and the other formations did eventually fragment, but this was not the whole story. Until the end of November 1944 the partisans had been gradually extending their hold on the province. They were pushing down the valleys into the foothills and disrupting enemy convoys on the Via Emilia and along the main road to Voghera. The rebels had even gone inside the city of Piacenza to capture the Fascist Prefect. He was taken to the mountains and forced to chop wood while chanting *'Duce, Duce.'*

The German and Fascist response was a great winter *rastrellamento,* or roundup. Instead of the sharp but short-lived forays of the past, they launched a large-scale military operation that crossed regional boundaries and lasted for months.

The offensive began in the province of Piacenza at dawn on 23 November. It was led by the 162nd Turkestan Infantry Division, which had German officers. They were supported by the Fascist *Bersagliere* Regiment. The force engaged the strongest partisan unit, the *Divisione Giustizia e Libertà*, to the north and north-west of the Tidone Valley.

The rebels were gradually pushed back into the Trebbia Valley. Their base at Bobbio was captured on the evening of 25 November. As there were also enemy troops at the mouth of the river the division was facing encirclement. The order was given for a general retreat towards the Nure. The local 60th and 61st brigades were commanded to hold positions on the right bank of the Trebbia to allow their comrades to escape. After three days the remaining partisans began to withdraw to a new defensive line in the mountains and Bettola fell on 2 December.

The Germans and Fascists had made a rapid advance of 100 kilometres. Inexplicably they then halted at the edge of the Arda Valley. The explanation is to be found in the War Diary of the 14th German Army. It reveals that its forces met such stubborn resistance between 23 November and 2 December that they were exhausted. Many detachments needed reorganising owing to heavy losses. Over the next five days Giuseppe Prati's partisans also conducted successful counter-attacks at the entrances to the Arda Valley with the help of some elements from the Nure Valley. The enemy halted on their positions for a month.

In the Nure Valley, the 60th and 61st brigades were dissolved and the squads mixed. On 12 December, the provincial military command created a new unit known as the *Settore Valnure*. It was to cater for men of all political beliefs and an experienced officer was drafted in from the Arda Valley to lead it: *Alpini* lieutenant Pietro Inzani, known as *Aquila Nera*. Second in command was 'Pippo,' Giuseppe Panni, and the Chief of Staff was Gian Maria Molinari, 'Gianmaria.'

A second phase of the enemy offensive began on 6 January 1945. *'Aquila Nera'* and 'Gianmaria' were both captured and shot. The *Settore Valnure* ceased to exist and the detachments once again became independent. However, the following month they regrouped in three new brigades.

Memorial to Lieutenant Pietro Inzani (*Aquila Nera*), awarded the Silver Medal as a martyr for Liberty, Monastero di Morfasso. (Cordani)

On 23 March the *Divisione Valnure* was created. It was led by 'Renato,' Pio Pietro Godoli, political commissar of the *Divisione Valdarda*. The brigades were named after the fallen commanders 'Inzani,' 'Gianmaria' and the Scotsman 'Mak.' The division played an important part in the final offensive that culminated in the liberation of Piacenza on 28 April.

NOTES

[1] Maria Carella Baio, *Le vere origini della Resistenza Piacentina*, pp 26-7.
[2] TNA: PRO HS 6/830, *Report by Capt. T. D. Gregg, Royal Tank Regiment*.
[3] See page 96 of my book, *Escape from Italy, 1943-45*.
[4] Baio, op. cit., p 151.
[5] TNA: PRO HS 6/830, Report ascribed to Lieutenant Commander A Gallegos, MBE. See Chapter Three in this book for the officer's escape through the lines.

8 THE MOST TRAVELLED ESCAPERS

Second Lieutenant William John Frank (Jack) Clarke from the RAOC was captured in north-eastern Libya on 8 April 1941 as Mekili was abandoned to the advancing German *Afrika Korps* after a three-day stand. In November 1942, he was transferred to the REME with the rank of lieutenant. The officer spent two and a half years as a prisoner in Italy: at Rezzanello and Montalbo in Piacenza and at the new camp at Fontanellato in Parma Province. After the war Jack Clarke wrote a brief account of his escape from the last camp. This is his story and that of some of his companions.

On 11 September 1943, the prisoners from PG 49 broke up into small groups. Many volunteered to work and after exchanging their battledress for civilian clothing were taken in twos and threes to local farms. Jack Clarke's companion was Costas Jacovides, a Greek Cypriot from Larnaka. He was serving in 1002 Pioneer Company, the Cyprus Regiment, and had been promoted to full lieutenant at Montalbo. The farm they were allocated was not to their liking: 'It was so bad,' wrote Jack Clarke, 'that we were soon fed up with the place and tried to get ourselves moved.'

For help they turned to Signorina Bianca Gelati, a district nurse from Fontanellato who visited her patients by bicycle. She had already brought the officers food and tins from Red Cross parcels and seemed well suited to act as unofficial billeting officer. Jack Clarke recalled:

> She made arrangements for us to go and stay at her house for a few days until some other plan could be made. We were very well looked after by Bianca and her sister, but it was soon apparent that they were very nervous and that we would not be able to remain there for long. She arranged for us to stay at a farm at Cannètolo with the Gotti family.
>
> The Germans had started putting up posters offering rewards to anyone who handed over a British POW and at the same time threatening considerable punishments to those who were caught harbouring one. In spite of these notices, the Italians did not as far as I know give up any prisoners.

Cannètolo is a little hamlet spread along the feeder road onto the *autostrada* to the west of Fontanellato. The farmhouse is a substantial building, painted yellow-ochre and surrounded by the usual barns and trees. The two officers stayed from 16 to 27 September, helping the family harvest beetroot and Indian corn. Each working day was a tonic after years of captivity. Jack Clarke related:

The food was good and plentiful and we had comfortable beds in which to sleep at night. Our midday meal was brought to us as we lay in the fields under the grapevines, as it was not considered advisable that we should be around the house during the day. Bianca came out from Fontanellato daily with newspapers and the latest local news. We listened to the BBC at nine o' clock in the evening. This was the first time we had heard Big Ben for about two and a half years. I scribbled down as much of the news as I could and passed it round next morning to other officers whom I knew were in the area.

The family called Jack Clarke 'Gianni.' One evening Signora Gotti cooked the two officers some meatballs. After they had savoured the meat and gravy, she said:

'Well, Gianni, were they nice?'
'Yes, delicious,' he replied.
'Do you know what they're made of? Horsemeat!'

Costas Jacovides's alias was Mario. He looked like an Italian and could speak the language fluently. He even went to the Sunday market in Fontanellato with the family, passing the time of day with the locals in the square.

On 20 September, the Germans launched the first of many raids on farms that were harbouring escaped prisoners of war and made several arrests. Gradually all the Allied servicemen were forced to reconsider their position, as Jack Clarke makes clear. Was it best to stay put, or to strike out for the Apennines or Switzerland?

We could have stayed on at the Gotti's indefinitely, but it became obvious to me that the British forces were not going to make any rapid advance up the Italian peninsula. At this time they were struggling for a very precarious foothold on the beaches of Salerno. It seemed to me that something had to be done. Jacovides was in favour of staying and waiting for the British to arrive. At the worst, he said, it would be a matter of a month or two. I reckoned about three to six months, which was too long for me to wait. In fact the Fifth Army arrived at the end of April 1945, nearly 20 months later.

As Jacovides would not come away at that time I looked for another travelling companion. Marcus Kane-Burman was seeking someone to join him and so we decided to set off together. [1]

Marcus Kane-Burman had joined the South African Medical Corps in 1940 and was captured with the rest of the Second Division at Tobruk two years later. Now a 40-year-old captain, he was the busy dentist at PG 49. Kane-Burman had promised to take one of his acting dental technicians with him, a Royal Navy rating by the name of McLean. 'So,' wrote Jack Clarke, 'the three of us agreed to push off south towards the Allied lines.' He continued:

There was much weeping at the Gotti farm when I announced my departure. They considered that I was very unwise and said that I could stay with them for as long as I liked. They had been most kind to me and I was sorry to leave them, but the possibility of a German roundup in the area seemed too great to allow me to go on endangering this family. The penalty for them would of course be much worse than for me in the event of my being rounded up ...

News had been brought in by Gordon Beazley (supposedly from the BBC) that Kesselring had detached some troops to stop the flow of prisoners who were making their way south. Subsequent events proved that this was only a rumour, but at the time we were rather impressed by it and promptly held another council of war. We decided that it would perhaps be better to make our way northwards and try to get into Switzerland. Having come to this decision we went to bed.

The three servicemen departed Cannètolo at five in the morning on Tuesday, 28 September, in steady drizzle. They crossed the railway line and the Via Emilia without incident and walked on to a welcoming farm at Costamezzana. The escapers dried their clothes in front of the fire and slept in the hayloft.

Wednesday dawned bright and the trio marched to Pellegrino Parmense where they found sanctuary at another farmstead. They met David Erskine and later John Dean and Gaston Vian [2] from Fontanellato on the way. Next morning the servicemen again moved off in fine weather, but left behind their one and only bar of Red Cross soap. They lunched at the roadside off haversack rations and hard-boiled eggs. Evening brought a billet in Metti, which was adequate but not quite so comfortable. Their friends Michael Ross and George Bell [3] paid them a surprise visit, apparently having been in the village for some time. Captain Kane-Burman earned his keep by pulling out a couple of teeth for members of the household.

On Friday morning the men woke to heavy rain. The going was heavier now in the hills of Piacenza and they were pleased to reach Morfasso at the top of the Arda Valley. It was difficult to find accommodation as many of the people feared local Fascists, but some of the villagers who could speak English helped find a suitable billet. Jack Clarke recalled:

> Here we decided that after all it would be a good thing to try to reach the British lines rather than to go to Switzerland. We determined to waste no more time, but to turn south on the following day.
>
> After we had gone to bed in our hayloft we were suddenly awakened by two people who were pointing revolvers at us. It appeared that we had been suspected of being the *Boche*. The investigators turned out to be none other than Branny Richards and Garrad-Cole whom I had known at Camp 17 [Rezzanello], so we had no difficulty in establishing our identity.

The escapers started their southward journey on Saturday, 2 October. They forded the River Ceno next day and followed ancient tracks into the high country along the Apennine ridge. 'On Wednesday,' Jack Clarke noted, 'we reached Scurano, where we met up with Pyman and Frazer [4] who had just arrived from Fontanellato by car. They told of the mopping up operations that the Germans had carried out in the area and of the capture of a number of 49-ers.' On two occasions the trio were taken to listen to the nine o' clock news on the wireless, but the reports were not encouraging as Allied progress was slow. On Saturday, 9 October, the walkers reached Gazzano at night and in pouring rain. They had been conducted by four elderly councillors returning home. Jack Clarke related:

On the way we met Finch, Abbott, Stephenson and Durrant [5], all 49-ers. At Gazzano we were split up between different houses and were well looked after. Our clothes were thoroughly dried out, and later washed and mended, other garments being loaned to us in the meantime.

We had decided to remain an extra day at Gazzano to have a rest and generally to get our kit put right. We didn't have any difficulty in persuading the people to let us stay, but we moved round to different houses for meals to lighten the load on any one family. We tried to get some decent maps from the priest, or from anyone who would give us one, but we had no success. We had been relying on the silk map up to now and though this was worth its weight in gold it didn't give much detail, nor was it very accurate. During our Sunday of rest at Gazzano, Gordon Dickens [6] and Squadron Leader Barr, an Australian from Camp 5 [Gavi], came through the village. So did several other 49-ers.

We left next day in bad weather - fine drizzle and mist - and had a new treat, 'elevenses.' We stopped at a wayside inn to enquire the way and were promptly offered a hot drink of coffee substitute, which was most welcome after the rain. We had to cut our trip short at about 3 o' clock in the afternoon as we were getting very high up on the slopes of Alpe Signetta and there was a definite danger of getting caught in a mist. We therefore stopped at a tiny hamlet known as Casa Piccirella, consisting of about three or four houses.

We had a guide for the last part of the trip - a good thing as it was hardly the type of country in which to get lost. Next day, Tuesday, 12 October, we had to cross the mountain, which rises to about 5,000 feet, and for this part of the journey we were again fortunate to have guides - a family with two mules returning to their home after a season of charcoal burning up in the hills.

The detailed account ends here, but from additional notes we see that the trio continued along the Apennines for another 38 days. On 4 November, they were worried by the presence of two furtive characters on a darkening hillside. They turned out to be their friends Richards and Garrad-Cole who had woken them up at gunpoint in Morfasso at the start of the journey.

On 8 November, Lieutenant Clarke, Captain Kane-Burman and Naval Rating McLean began to walk in snow. Nine days later they reached the small village of Santa Maria in Abruzzo, where other escapers were already resting and recuperating ready for the final push. These included Captain Geoffrey Phalp and Lieutenant Gervase Nicholls, both from the Royal Artillery, who had left another farm in the Fontanellato area two days after their colleagues. They moved together to Frattura, gateway to Monte Greco, the hills overlooking the River Sangro and friendly forces. But next day, Friday, 19 November, Clarke, Kane-Burman and McLean were captured by German troops within sight of Allied positions. It was 300 miles as the crow flies from Fontanellato. As the journey progressed the men had become used to covering longer distances. Usually they remained just one night. The trio stayed at 44 different places during their march south.

Captain Phalp and Lieutenant Nicholls made a successful crossing at dawn the following day. They were able to report what had happened to the others. In Frattura the escapers had met an Italian guide who said that he had already taken several parties through the lines. Early next morning they joined a large group, which followed him up snowy crags in a winding column. It was a slow climb and there was a lot of noise. Phalp and Nicholls decided to go off on their own, but half an hour later heard shouting and gunfire. The main party had been ambushed by a German patrol.

The captives were taken across the regional border into Lazio and held in a transit camp in the provincial capital of Frosinone. On 30 November they were entrained for Germany, but several managed to escape during the journey. It was on the main line to Florence near Orte in the province of Viterbo, still in Lazio, 83 kilometres north of Rome.

Jack Clarke reported to the War Office on the breakout from the prison train in April 1945 when he was back in England. He said there were 26 officers in his cattle truck, of whom at least 8 had escaped. As well as the lieutenant himself, these included Captain Kane-Burman, SAMC, Major Hugh Fane-Hervey, MC,

RTR, Captain Donald Macaulay, RAMC, Lieutenant Anthony Laing, RE, and Flight Lieutenant Garrad-Cole. We will follow the adventures of all of these officers.

'Details of the escape are as follows,' wrote Jack Clarke:

An axe, which had been taken from the Germans in the POW camp at Frosinone, was concealed and taken into the train. After the train had started, the wall of the cattle truck was cut partly through by means of the axe, it being intended to complete the hole after dark. On the first night, however, 3-4 December, the train remained stationary in Rome station all night and no escape was possible.

On the next night, 4-5 December, the train started at about 1.30am and the work of cutting the hole was immediately completed. Just before 2am I escaped, a number of others having already gone in the previous few minutes. The hole was made in the forward end of the truck over the coupling. The escape was made by climbing onto the coupling and then the buffers and jumping clear. The train was moving at about 15 to 20 miles per hour at the time.

The truck in which I was held was placed immediately in front of the passenger coach holding the German guards. There were also guards in a number of the brakeman's boxes on the ends of the goods trucks. Whenever the train stopped, these guards would immediately alight from their carriage and spread themselves out along both sides of the train until it restarted. It was thus more or less impossible to escape while the train was stationary, or in daylight, owing to the proximity of the coach carrying the guards.

Immediately after jumping from the truck I walked along the track and rejoined Lieutenant Laing, who had jumped in front of me. We then remained hidden until daylight, after which we continued on our way to Florence.

The city was a considerable distance away, 233 kilometres. The two lieutenants found sanctuary at a nearby Franciscan monastery and were provided with money and food for the days ahead. They took a train journey on 9 December. Four days later the officers were just north-east of the Tuscan capital in the hill village of Santa Brigida. Lieutenant Laing had previously been given a warm welcome there on his way south at the holiday home of Signor Leopoldo Tarchiani, a prosperous Florentine silk merchant. He drove them down to the city on Tuesday, 21 December. They were sheltered by the Valvona-Buti family. The industrialist father was interned in England as an enemy alien. His wife, Pamela, had been born of Italian parents in Britain. She lived with her two children and an Austrian Governess at 8, Via Ciro Menotti, a solid two-storey apartment built in the Palladian style. Over a seven-month period the family helped 14 escaped prisoners of war. Mario Nappini assisted in the work, providing the men with food and money and the benefit of his extensive contacts.

Jack Clarke and Anthony Laing lived in the flat for most of the two months up to 21 February 1944. Another prisoner had been in residence since November, a South African artillery officer, Captain Erland Hindson.

Jack Clarke's notes record that they lunched with Signor Tarchiani on 5 January and attended the opera *La Bohème* next day. Three days later they were joined by Captain EH (Ted) Mumford of the 3 Gurkha Rifles, Indian Army. He had made his way south from another farm at Fontanellato with the writer and broadcaster Stuart Hood, then a captain in the Highland Light Infantry.

Mumford and Hood had joined a partisan group on Monte Morello, which dominates the landscape north of Florence. In the New Year of 1944 Ted Mumford left on a mission to recover mortar casings with two partisans. On 3 January, Stuart Hood and the other fighters settled for the night in a barn at Valibona as snow began to fall. No sentries were posted. Early morning light revealed Fascist militia in platoon strength climbing the hillside. After a firefight which lasted two hours the partisan commander, Lanciotto Ballerini, and two of his men had been killed and eight captured. Four escaped from the burning barn, including Stuart Hood. He went on to serve as area commander for another partisan group, a more professional outfit led by former army officers and based in 'Chiantishire.' Finally the captain was sent into Siena to liase with Allied troops once the city fell. This turned out to be on 3 July. The two friends did not meet again in Italy.

Jack Clarke, Anthony Laing and Ted Mumford managed to obtain genuine identity cards through a Signora Amendola and began to plan their final escape. They left Florence by train at ten to six on the evening of 22 January 1944 for an overnight journey to Venice, 257 kilometres away. They were led by a Communist called Angelo Salvatore. He spent most of his time in the train corridor on the look out for potential danger. The officers travelled in separate compartments so that if one was arrested it would not compromise the others. The aim was to reach the Yugoslav border, make contact with the Slovenian partisans, and cross the Adriatic by boat. If this proved impossible, there were rumours of night time pickups by Allied craft along the Venetian Gulf.

The escapers booked into the Albergo Rialto in the San Marco district of Venice for two nights. This superior hotel is housed in an ancient palace a few yards from the Rialto Bridge, with splendid views over the Grand Canal. When the trio came down for breakfast next day they were waved to the only empty table at the far end of the dining room. Looking round, they discovered that all the other guests were German staff officers. Even so, the decision was made to remain for a second night. It was thought that the hotel was the last place the Germans would suspect the presence of British officers. And so it proved.

However, the men were unable to make contact with any escape organisation in the city and they moved by train to Padua. They stayed in a guesthouse for two nights, but when the prospects in this city proved to be as dismal, they were forced to return to Florence. The three friends arrived on 27 January after a journey by train and tram and went back to the apartment.

Jack Clarke noted that they made another visit to the opera on 6 February. It was again to see a performance of Puccini, this time *Madam Butterfly*.

A fortnight later the officers and Angelo Salvatore were on the move once more. They left Florence by train on 21 February, travelled overnight, arrived in Milan at a quarter to two in the afternoon and stayed at a small hotel. In the morning the trio followed Angelo at a discrete distance to the *Stazione Nord*. He bought them tickets for the local train to Laveno on the eastern shore of Lake Maggiore and gave final instructions.

The officers crossed by ferry to Cannero Riviera as directed and went up the lakeside by bus to Cannobio. They knocked at the back door of a café and gave the owner a password. At dusk he pointed them along the mule track up the Cannobina Valley to Socraggio. There two guides came forward once another password provided at the café was given. They were well used to secret trails and dodging the authorities as *contrabbandieri*, or smugglers.

'At 5 in the morning on 24 February,' Jack Clarke wrote, 'we departed and arrived at the peak at 11.55. We crossed the frontier and gave ourselves up to Swiss frontier guards at 15.30 hours.' [7] Anthony Laing recalled:

We left at dawn and, like all good Italian businessmen, in gents' natty city suits and shoes and carrying briefcases, we slipped and slithered our way up to a col, which we were assured was the Swiss frontier, and where we said goodbye to our guides. We descended similarly on the other side and, having just reached the tree line, were happily and carelessly talking when a voice behind us called 'Alt!' Turning, I saw a German soldier in the usual field grey uniform. My heart sank. Had we failed again? But no, he was a Swiss soldier. [8]

On 1 March, the flat in Florence was raided by the Fascist Secret Police. Pamela Buti was taken away together with Captain Erland Hindson. The next day the son, Kim, was also captured. Pamela was eventually liberated when partisans stormed the prison in which she was held to release one of their agents. She then ensured her son was freed from a forced labour detachment by bribing a German guard with her wedding ring, a gold watch and money provided by the Resistance.

For actions during the period between the escape from Fontanellato and rejoining Allied forces, Jack Clarke gained a Mention in Despatches, Anthony Laing was awarded the MC, and Stuart Hood the MBE.

Ted Mumford returned to his battalion on the Italian front and once the campaign was over visited the farm at Toccalmatto where he and Stuart Hood began their journey. From behind a family photograph on the wall the son reached down a gold ring. The officer had given it to him for safe keeping, saying he would collect it 'after the war.'

* * *

Following the escape from the German prison train at Orte on 5 December, Captain Marcus Kane-Burman teamed up with another of the successful officers, Captain Donald Macaulay, RAMC, also a medic from Fontanellato. They were seen next day by a different group of escapers: Major d'Arcy Mander, of the Green Howards, from PG 29 Veano, and South African lieutenants Jack Selikman and Sandy Stewart, from PG 47 Modena. They remembered two ragged figures sloshing over wet fields in the opposite direction. A *'Buon giorno'* received only a muttered reply as they passed. All of sudden there was a shout:

'Marcus!'
'Jack!' and 'Good Lord, Sandy!'

Jack Selikman had recognised his dentist from home in Johannesburg. The two groups met again four times before reaching Rome. Through the doctors, Major Mander and the South Africans were put in touch with an Italian at Soriano who provided shelter and sent them with two guides to Vignanello. From there they were taken by train to the capital on 9 December. With other escapers the trio were accommodated and looked after by the British Organisation for Assisting Allied Escaped Prisoners of War in the Via Chelini flat. A few days later Kane-Burman and Macaulay walked in. However, the apartment was betrayed, and raided by the Gestapo on 8 January. Fourteen officers, a sergeant and two helpers were arrested.

Major Mander escaped. He had returned to the flat after the raid had taken place and was bundled into the front room by two German guards as they awaited further callers. They did not bother to check a shuttered window and the major was able to vault through it to the street below. He went on to form his own intelligence network and was awarded the DSO 'for the courage and resource shown during his undercover operations in the city.' [9]

The other residents of the Via Chelini flat were sent to the infamous Regina Coeli ('Queen of Heaven') prison. As the captives were in civilian clothing they were suspected of being enemy spies. Only the intervention of the Red Cross saved them from torture or even the firing squad. When their true status had been established the men were entrained for camps in Germany on 26 January.

Captain Kane-Burman and Lieutenant Selikman managed to break out of their cattle wagon once the train had crossed the heavily defended Po River bridge into Lombardy. Five weeks later the officers escaped to Switzerland. They arrived on 1 March, only five days after Jack Clarke, Anthony Laing and Ted Mumford.

Lieutenant Jack Clarke. Top left: Italian passport photograph, January 1944. Top right: Outside Florence, December 1943. Below: Arosa, Switzerland, August 1944. (Rosemary Clarke)

Marcus Kane-Burman became Senior Dental Officer for the large Allied escaper and evader community in the Confederation. On 1 March 1945, he was awarded the MBE for services to his fellow prisoners of war in Italy.

* * *

The officer who obtained the axe for the prison train breakout was Major Hugh Fane-Hervey. He had won the Military Cross fighting the Italians at Sidi Barrani aged 24 and led the 'Other Ranks' company during the escape from Fontanellato.

The major had also taken the road to Rome. He was accompanied by Flight Lieutenant Garrad-Cole, whom we last encountered in the Apennines in November. One of the priests helping the Allied escape organisation persuaded the caretaker at the Swiss Legation to let the officers use an apartment in a closed off section of the building, which was formerly the British Embassy. The major again used his ingenuity in breaking into the sealed off wine cellar and the two friends celebrated the Christmas of 1943 in some style. They moved later to avoid compromising the diplomatic status of the British Minister, Sir D' Arcy Osborne.

The two officers stayed in a variety of private billets. Early one morning, at the flat of Renzo and Adrienne Lucidi in Via Scialoia, Major Fane-Hervey was awoken by a German trooper shouting 'Light! Light!' When the soldier demanded to know who he was the Englishman muttered the first thing that came into his head, which was 'Paula.' The German nodded, looked around for a moment or two, and left. The troops were also taken in by another lodger, Lieutenant William Simpson, who told them he was Adrienne's nephew. When the confused Germans returned, the officers had fled.

After a brief and unsuccessful attempt to cross the lines at Anzio, Flight Lieutenant Garrad-Cole returned to Rome. At six foot four inches tall and blond he stood out in a crowd. One day the airman was followed off a tram and along the street by two uniformed Germans. They demanded to see his identity card, which was forged, and gave him an order. The airman understood only two words, Via Tasso,' the location of the Gestapo headquarters. As they marched along, the officer stuck his leg out and tripped one of the guards. The other released a random shot as Garrad-Cole fled around a corner and into a familiar block. On the top floor was the Lucidi's flat. The fugitive re-emerged some time later, with a change of coat and hat and hand in hand with the family's eleven-year-old son, Maurice, who chattered away to him in Italian. They passed the German soldiers unchallenged.

The commander of the British network in Rome, Major Sam Derry, remarked that this was 'an example of something we had always believed: that if the Germans were told to look for a tall man in a light raincoat and a dark hat, they would never think of stopping a tall man in a dark raincoat and a light hat.'

Major Fane-Hervey adopted the alias of Count Paolo Fattorini. He regularly attended the Rome Opera House and hired a box next to that of the German Commander. On one occasion the major even obtained the German's autograph on his programme.

When the capital was freed in June 1944, Hugh Fane-Hervey captured five Germans and handed them over to the Allies. He was awarded a Bar to the Military Cross that he had won in the deserts of North Africa.

During the previous nine months Rome and the Vatican City had been a magnet for escapers and evaders from all over central and northern Italy. The official British Organisation in Rome for Assisting Allied Escaped Prisoners of War is the topic of the next chapter.

NOTES

[1] Lieutenant Costas Jacovides was among the escaped prisoners of war my family helped. He remained in the area for over a year and crossed the lines in the autumn of 1944. See my book, *British Prisoners of War in Italy: Paths to Freedom.*

[2] Captain DB Erskine, RTR, from Fontanellato. He was recaptured; lieutenants Gaston Vian and John Dean, both RA, and also from PG 49. See my book, *Escape from Italy, 1943-45,* for their escape to Switzerland.

[3] Captain Michael Ross, the Welch Regiment, and Lieutenant Cecil (George) Bell, Highland Light Infantry. They escaped to Monte Carlo. Michael Ross is the author of *From Liguria with Love,* published by Minerva Press of London in 1997.

[4] Major HD Pyman, the Sherwood Foresters, and Captain KA Frazer, RAOC, both from Fontanellato. The captain was recaptured while trying to cross the Swiss border on 23 December 1943.

[5] Captain RJ Finch, Major Denny Abbott, Captain Theo. Stephenson and Major Noel Durrant, all Indian Army.

[6] Second Lieutenant Gordon Dickens, RAC, from Fontanellato.

[7] Information credit: Rosemary Clarke, Leamington Spa.

[8] Ian English, ed., *Home by Christmas?* pp 60-1.

[9] See d' Arcy Mander, *Mander's March on Rome,* published in 1987, and Chapter Seven in my book, *Escape from Italy, 1943-45.*

In the Alps. (Kydd)

9 *VENI CREATOR SPIRITUS*

In September 1943, Hitler intended to send a force to occupy the Vatican, kidnap Pope Pius XII and put the state treasures and archives in storage. The SS commander in Italy, General Wolff, was summoned to the Wolf's Lair to discuss urgent plans for the occupation. He managed to dissuade the Führer on the grounds that the 3,000 troops necessary for the takeover could not be spared and that it would cause serious unrest in Italy and condemnation abroad.

The general was able to tell His Holiness that he was in no imminent danger. The German Ambassador, Count Ernst von Weizsäcker, added that 'the sovereignty and territorial integrity of the Vatican will be respected and furthermore the Germans undertake to conduct themselves in such a way to protect the Vatican City from the fighting.' However, the threat of occupation still remained. The Papacy had to maintain a precarious balancing act between Germany and the Allied powers.

Before the Armistice of September 1943, five Allied servicemen entered the Vatican and were interned. Four were later sent home in a prisoner exchange with the Italians. On the Armistice another seven fugitives managed to evade the Papal gendarmes. Fearing the city-state would be swamped the Vatican authorities then ordered that all would-be internees were to be repelled at the gates.

Thousands of Allied escapers and evaders still took the road to Rome. Fortunately, many of the fugitives made for the closed British Embassy. The caretaker, Secondo Constantini, directed them to offices within the building used by the Swiss Legation. The Military Attaché, Captain Leonardo Trippi, was already known to many of the men through his inspection visits to camps. He gave the servicemen money and Red Cross parcels and told them about the secret emergency committee set up for their welfare.

Overseeing the operation was Sir D' Arcy Osborne, British Minister to the Holy See. Like all the other diplomats of the anti-Axis countries he resided in the Santa Marta barracks, an austere four-storey building just inside the Vatican. The ground floor was taken up by Papal offices and the other levels were occupied by the refugee legations. The British were at the very top.

The network was run by a shadowy Council of Three. So as not to compromise his diplomatic status, Sir D' Arcy entrusted day to day arrangements to his butler, John May, a cheerful Londoner with a wide circle of contacts.

The leader of the group was the Right Reverend Monsignor Hugh O' Flaherty, a citizen of the neutral Irish Free State. He was tall, with twinkling blue eyes and round metal-rimmed spectacles. The priest, who later would become known as 'The Scarlet Pimpernel of the Vatican,' was a keen boxer and golfing champion. He was a Notary of the Holy Office and had already served as a diplomat and as secretary and interpreter to the Papal Nuncio to the camps in Italy. The monsignor was dismissed from his role under Italian Government pressure at the end of 1942. He had taken Red Cross parcels and books to the captives and returned with their details for transmission on Vatican Radio. The English language announcer was Father Owen Sneddon, a New Zealander. His broadcasts ensured that the families of thousands of Allied servicemen knew that they were 'missing - but known to be safe.'

The priest's apartment was in one of the extraterritorial properties on the left-hand fringe of the Vatican complex. The ancient *Collegio Teutonicum*, or German College, had once been a hostel for Germans on pilgrimage, but was now a centre for the study of Church history and archaeology. Most of the residents were actual Germans, but they were Christians not Nazis. Next door is the Palace of the Holy Office and on the other side in the Vatican proper is Santa Marta. The monsignor had a small downstairs office and it became a clearinghouse for Jews and anti-Fascists wanted by the Italian State. A few of the fugitives were retained in the German College and the rest were sent to other Vatican properties in Rome and to private houses. Now the humanitarian effort was broadened to include Allied escapers and evaders.

The final member of the Council of Three was Count Sarsfield Salazar. His father had been ennobled by the Italian King in 1905 when Consul General in Dublin. The count was a British Subject and served as a cavalry officer in its army during the First World War. He was briefly interned by the Italians in 1940 and subsequently acted as a prisoner of war camp inspector for the protecting powers, initially the United States and then Switzerland. Salazar was soon denounced and his apartment raided, but he went undercover and helped coordinate what became known as the country branch of the Rome Organisation. At the time his son, Juan, was serving with the Chindits in Burma.

He was awarded an immediate Military Cross in 1944 for single handedly destroying a Japanese fuel dump.

New arrivals were entrusted to the care of a Maltese widow called Henrietta Chevalier, who lived with her mother and five children in a small flat at 12, Via Imperia. After a few weeks it seemed as if the Rome Organisation would be overwhelmed. As the number of servicemen increased the monsignor rented flats at Via Firenze and Via Chelini. The prisoners, or 'packages' as they were called, were given new clothing, escorted to their lodgings and provided with money for subsistence. The escape line now had contact with over a thousand escapers and evaders.

In the middle of November, the Council received a fortuitous note sent via a village priest and a courier. It was simply addressed to 'Anyone English in the Vatican,' and read: 'To whom it may concern. There are a group of Allied prisoners beyond Salone in urgent need of financial assistance and clothing.' The plea was signed 'S.I. Derry, major.'

The officer was sent 3,000 lire in notes. Four days later the priest came to the capital and handed over a receipt from the soldier, an expression of thanks and a request for more funds. Another payment was made, but this time it was accompanied by a summons to meet the priest's superior in Rome.

Twenty nine-year-old Major Samuel Ironmonger Derry, MC, from the Royal Artillery, had been head of the escape committee at PG 21 Chieti. Following the Armistice the officers were sent to Sulmona and eventually entrained for Germany. At 8.30 the following morning the major made a successful jump from the train. At nightfall he approached a lonely smallholding, made friends with the farmer and his wife and spent the night in their straw stack.

Sam Derry awoke to the sight of the majestic dome of Saint Peter's less than 20 miles away on the horizon. He intended to move southwards and link up with Allied forces. However, when the major found himself the only officer among a group of 50 Allied escapers he was forced to change his plans. He felt obliged to do something for the men and had asked the local priest if it was possible to send a message to the Vatican.

Major Derry was smuggled into the capital on Saturday, 20 November. He was concealed among a load of cabbages on a pony cart bound for market. The officer was taken to meet Monsignor O' Flaherty in Saint Peter's Square and conducted to his lodgings. The two men were of similar height at over six foot. Disguised in a set of the priest's robes, the major followed him into the Vatican for a meal with the British Minister. Sam Derry recollected the encounter in his fine memoir, *The Rome Escape Line*, published in 1960:

> 'Your note signed 'S.I. Derry, major,' was the first contact we had made with a senior British officer,' Sir D' Arcy told me. 'When the monsignor saw that in one breath you had thanked him for the money and asked him for more he was highly amused and decided on the spot that you were the man to take control of the organisation. That is why we sent for you.
>
> 'I must tell you that I consider the monsignor's efforts have been absolutely wonderful, but he feels, and I agree, that the time has come now when we must appoint somebody to coordinate all the work. It will not be easy and I am afraid it is likely to get more difficult as time goes on. Now that you know what it is all about, are you prepared to take command?' [1]

Sam Derry agreed, as long as he was first able to return to the escapers in the countryside. He put non-commissioned officers in charge, distributed money and told the men to stay put for the time being. The officer returned to Rome concealed in another load of cabbages and had a further meeting with the minister. Sir D' Arcy had sent a coded message to Britain requesting background information on Derry. Now the knight interrogated the soldier on life in his hometown of Newark in Nottinghamshire. Derry recalled:

> My answers apparently satisfied him and with that the official British Organisation in Rome for Assisting Allied Escaped Prisoners of War was born: a unique military unit, the like of which may never be seen again ... The aim was straightforward if not simple ... to build up an organisation capable of keeping the constantly growing numbers of escapers converging on the Rome area out of enemy hands. That meant finding places for the men to live, ensuring that they regularly received food, clothing and medical supplies, and, where possible, concentrating them in relatively 'safe' coastal areas for evacuation by British 'cloak and dagger' forces. [2]

The minister explained that in Rome most food had to be obtained through the black market. Supplies were becoming scarce and the situation would become worse over the course of the winter. So men were to be kept out of the city as far as possible. Those who did reach the capital needed to be provided with temporary accommodation and then gradually moved out in groups to the surrounding countryside.

Sir D' Arcy also made clear that he would be unable to give much direct help apart from organising funds from secret British Government sources. However, he was able to provide three of the interned officers to act as a registry or secretariat. They were: Captain Henry Judson Byrnes, a Canadian, Major John Munroe Sym of the Seaforth Highlanders and Sub Lieutenant Roy Charlton Elliot from the Royal Navy. An extensive card index system was developed that provided an outline history of all but a few of the Allied prisoners of war in Italy.

Major Derry took up residence in the monsignor's apartment at the German College. The officer's cover was that he was Patrick Derry, a native of Dublin, working as a writer for the Holy See. The priest supplied him with a genuine Vatican identity card.

Derry visited all the safe houses and placed the senior man in each in charge, laying down an evacuation routine which would not compromise the hosts, the *padroni*, in case of raids. While recaptured servicemen would be sent to camps, the Germans had imposed the death penalty for harbouring escapers and evaders. The threat was repeated every day on German-controlled Rome Radio and in the newspapers.

For the first time, contact was established with Allied forces in the south. The British escape and evasion agency sent an agent to Rome, unaware what was already being done. 'My difficulty,' Derry recalled, 'was that one could scarcely ask an MI 9 man for his credentials. The monsignor, in whatever way my questions were phrased, simply said, "Why, me boy, I know him well," and changed the subject.'

The operative, Pier Luigi Tumiati (Peter), a young bilingual journalist from Milan, was asked to carry information back to Bari in liberated territory. He left with the names, service numbers and ranks of almost 2,000 ex prisoners known to be at large. The lists were microfilmed and baked inside a small loaf by John May. A coded message on the BBC a few weeks later confirmed that 'Peter' had safely rejoined friendly forces. He went on to help create an escape route through the lines and to organise naval rescues on the east coast.

Meanwhile, intermediaries had introduced another agent to Major Derry, whom he described as 'one of my most valuable contacts.' Dashing Italian paratroop major Umberto Losena was dropped near Rome to open radio contact with the south. The officer also volunteered to carry supplies to Allied servicemen in Lazio and Umbria two or three times a week.

Four RAF supply drops were arranged to two of the largest country groups of servicemen at Montorio Romano and Nerola. Three naval pickups were also organised from the Adriatic coast. Popski's Private Army guarded the evacuations, but several hundred men were taken south on infantry landing craft without the need for a shot to be fired.

Eventually the source of the broadcasts was traced and Major Losena was captured. He was one of 5 helpers belonging to the Rome Organisation among 320 Italians executed in the Ardeatine Caves massacre in March 1944, savage reprisal for a Communist bomb in the Via Rasella which killed 32 German troops.

The Rome Organisation was only one of the international underground groups operating in the capital. But all the others looked to Derry for instructions as the sole Allied commander in the city, wrongly believing he was in direct contact with the armies in the south. He was, he said, 'the honorary president of a sort of United Nations conglomeration of kindred societies.'

Two senior diplomats ran the 'Free French' movement from the collaborationist Vichy Embassy. There were Italian nobles and left wingers and Yugoslav royalists and Communists.

The smallest but most daring group was Greek. It was named 'Liberty or Death' and was financed by the British. One of its leaders was an escaped prisoner of war called Theodore Meletiou (Mario). He visited Major Derry and said that during a secret journey to the north in search of his fugitive countrymen he had made contact near Arezzo with the most senior group of Allied escapers in Italy, led by General Philip Neame, VC. The agent offered to guide the men to Rome, but the major told him it would be prudent to bring just one. 'Mario' returned a month later, in mid January, with Major General Gambier-Parry, MC, and Mrs Mary Boyd, a Scottish internee who was in danger for having helped escaped prisoners of war. The general declined an offer from Derry of assuming command of the organisation and was placed in secure accommodation in the home of a noblewoman of

British birth. However, the monsignor became aware that the officer was growing bored, as Derry recalled:

As Chief of Staff of this artful dodger, I ordered all our escapers to stay undercover lest they compromise the Italian *padroni* who courted death by harbouring them.

Yet the gravest security problems were posed by the monsignor himself. He delighted in flirting with danger. After we'd long kept a British general cooped up in a secret room, O' Flaherty took that star boarder out to a Papal reception, garbed in Donegal tweeds, and introduced him as an Irish doctor to the German Ambassador!

Sam Derry quickly found the general a new billet. He became a 'patient' of the Little Sisters of Mary at San Stefano Rotondo, with plenty of space to exercise in the grounds, and remained there safely until the liberation.

In March 1944, the Greek leader, Evanghelos Averoff, and 'Mario' were loaned a car by a turncoat Fascist and obtained all the necessary documents for travel. They decided on a grand tour of the north. Derry was pleased as he was finding it difficult to deliver supplies to the area. In one district he was entirely reliant on a woman with a donkey for distribution to more than 80 Allied servicemen. The Greeks took 100,000 lire, clothing, boots and a miniature camera. They returned three weeks later after travelling as far as Milan and motoring over 2,000 miles. The pair had contacted dozens of groups of escapers, given out money and supplies and collected information. They brought lists of servicemen and their next of kin, intelligence on German troop dispositions and photographs of a line of defence along the border with France.

By the beginning of December 1943, the number of escapers and evaders supported in the countryside had grown to more than 2,000, with another 80 in Rome. A modest 120 lire a day was originally paid out to the *padroni* inside Rome in respect of each serviceman and substantially less in the countryside. In the six weeks up to 9 December 69,000 lire were distributed, but in another month the figure reached the million mark. By March 1944 costs were running at two million lire a month, or over a thousand pounds a week.

The Rome Organisation was a major player in the city's black market. Sam Derry said that its activities were a crucial factor in the collapse of the official rationing system. British expenditure on illicit clothing was 107,000 lire in January 1944 and 187,000 lire by March. The network's agents even bought American cigarettes that had been captured by the Germans. The recipients included some of the people for whom the packets were originally intended, United States servicemen. About 1,500 had been taken prisoner of war either before or after September 1943.

Fortunately, the British Treasury agreed to meet Sir D' Arcy Osborne's 'crying and urgent' demands for money for British former prisoners of war, wherever they were in Italy and even without the usual paperwork.

The accounting system of the Rome Organisation consisted of a school exercise book with the simplest of entries: a date, codename and sum of money, cross-referenced where possible with basic receipts. Each contact was given a pseudonym: Sam Derry was Patrick, the monsignor was Golf, Count Salazar was Emma and Mrs Chevalier became Mrs M. The alias of the British Minister, Mount, and that of his secretary, Hugh Montgomery, Till, were not even written down. The records were buried in the Vatican gardens each evening in sealed biscuit tins. The possibility of German raids could never be completely discounted. In March 1944, receipts were abandoned altogether on grounds of security. The billeting officers' reports were ruled sufficient to sign off the vast sums of money required.

The American *Chargé d' Affaires*, Harold Tittman, contributed towards the costs of United States nationals helped by the escape line, mainly downed aircrew. The extraterritorial American College, located on Janiculum Hill near to the Vatican, was the only major billet used by the organisation that was not raided. Prince Doria Pamphili led a group of noble benefactors and made a personal donation of 150,000 lire. The prince became Mayor of Rome on the liberation.

Officers were sometimes able to make their own financial arrangements with private citizens, obtaining Italian lire in exchange for cheques drawn on British banks which could only be honoured at the end of hostilities. No doubt some of these lucky individuals were among the British officers reported in a Fascist newspaper as eating expensive meals in fashionable restaurants while the poor of Rome were almost starving.

On 8 December 1943, reinforcements for the escape line arrived in the shape of three of Derry's companions from the camp at Sulmona: Private Joseph Pollak of the Palestine Pioneer

Company and gunnery lieutenants John Furman and William Simpson. Pollak was of Czech origin and in civilian life had been a medical student. He was a fluent linguist and mixed easily with the Italians. The officers shared a financial background, Furman as a chartered accountant and Simpson as an employee of the Royal Insurance Company. But they were opposites in appearance and temperament, which may explain the success of their partnership. Furman was a diminutive, dapper southerner while Simpson was a tall, upright Scot.

Priests found most of the new lodgings, but the trio became the organisation's billeting officers, guiding servicemen to their accommodation, issuing money and distributing supplies. Food bought on the black market by Mrs Chevalier was ferried to safe houses in horse drawn cabs. The lieutenants went to stay with Renzo and Adrienne Lucidi and in between assignments enjoyed Rome's social life to the full, mixing with Germans and Fascists in restaurants and at the opera.

Christmas 1943 was celebrated with the payment of small amounts of extra money for the men to buy supplementary food and comforts. A dinner was held in the monsignor's apartment, as Derry recalled:

> He always ate frugally, and Christmas dinner, served by the German sisters, who now accepted me with something like affection as the Irish Patrick Derry, was no great gastronomic experience, but at a time when meat was very scarce, even a slice of mutton was most welcome, if hardly festive. Certainly there was nothing sparse about the cheerful goodwill that flowed about the monsignor's room throughout that day and it seemed to me that visitors were in and out in a never ending procession. There were priests of half a dozen nationalities, who were all helping in the organisation's work, diplomats and their families from the French, Polish, Yugoslav and other legations, Mrs Kiernan and her two daughters from the Irish Embassy and a large number of unusual characters who had been in hiding in various parts of the college since before my arrival. [3]

The year's end brought the reduction of the curfew to seven o' clock, the closing of the door onto the street from the German College - leaving the only pathway a gate overseen by a Swiss

Guard post - and the news of the arrest of helpers in my family's home valley of the Arda.

On 6 January 1944, Private Pollak was lured to the flat of a young Italian woman, 'Iride,' who had brought him and the two other billeting officers to Rome together with another four escapers. 'Iride' had been captured by the Germans and forced to betray her contacts. The Gestapo were waiting for Pollak and he was arrested and taken back to Sulmona together with the woman and her sister, Maria. An entire helper network that had been carefully nurtured by Derry was rounded up in the city and a dozen escapers arrested.

Two days later, the transit flats at Via Chelini and Via Firenze were raided by the German SS, but Major Mander managed to escape from Via Chelini, as we saw in the last chapter. William Simpson was warned by the janitor from entering the building and was able to go to the Vatican and tell Major Derry: 'Via Chelini's fallen.'

Lieutenant Furman was among the captives taken to the Regina Coeli gaol. The raid was the result of denunciation by the cook of a Communist leader called Nebolante, whom the Germans had arrested and threatened.

On 23 January, Sam Derry received a note from John Furman that had been smuggled out of the prison by an Italian barber. The lieutenant listed his companions as the two officers who had been staying at Nebolante's flat, Lieutenant 'Tug' Wilson, DSO, and Captain 'Pip' Gardner, VC, MC, and captains Macaulay and Kane-Burman, lieutenants Stewart and Selikman, and 'other ranks' Billet, Knox-Davies, Gibb, Churchill, Hands and Eaton, an American. A further letter from Furman two days later said that he had just been given the news that all the British prisoners were about to be sent north in two or three hours time.

The religious helpers were also under constant threat. SS Lieutenant Colonel Herbert Kappler made several attempts to kidnap Monsignor O' Flaherty. Once he was surrounded in the palace of Prince Pamphili and sped past his would-be captors in a coal dray. Another time, the priest rugby-tackled his pursuers and dived into the extraterritorial Santa Maria Maggiore.

Finally, Monsignor O' Flaherty was invited to a reception at the Hungarian Embassy. The German Ambassador, Baron von Weizsäcker, accosted him and said:

'Nobody in Rome honours you more than I for what you are doing. But it has gone too far for all of us. Kappler is waiting in the hall, feeling rather frustrated. I have told him that you will of course have safe conduct back to the Vatican tonight. But if you ever step outside Vatican territory again on whatever pretext you will be arrested at once. Now will you think about what I have said?

'Your Excellency is too considerate,' replied O' Flaherty. 'I will certainly think about what you have said - sometimes!'

However, the threat was followed up by an official caution from the Vatican Secretariat and Hugh O' Flaherty was then forced to remain inside the city-state and to delegate his outside interests to other priests.

Shortly afterwards, the monsignor told Derry that the College Rector had become aware that 'Patrick' was not a neutral Irishman and that he would have to leave at once. In addition, the Germans knew that he was aiding escaped prisoners of war.

After consulting the minister, the major adopted a new alias of Toni and disappeared into the Legation's apartments. He became, in his own words, 'The Ghost of the Vatican,' a diplomatic secret, the only Allied serviceman within the city-state who was not interned.

The Allied landings at Anzio on 22 January had a negative overall impact on the organisation. A few small groups of escapers south of the city were able to reach the bridgehead within the first confused twenty-four hours. Afterwards, the German counter-attack prevented any movement and Rome became a front line base for divisions from all over northern Italy. In addition, adverse weather conditions virtually blocked the escape line south. Major Derry told the United States *Chargé d' Affaires* that ex prisoners sent along the route had all returned, reporting that:

(a) It is practically impossible to obtain food when some distance from the lines.

(b) Snow on the mountain slopes makes going very slow.

(c) They have seen several British ex prisoners of war, especially Indians, dead on the mountains, apparently having died of exposure or hunger.

In February, the number of servicemen on the organisation's books rose by 338 to 2,591, in spite of recaptures, two or three hundred men who escaped to Switzerland and a few who crossed the lines. The figure for the capital grew from 84 to 116. By mid March the total of escapers and evaders had increased to 3,423, with 180 now in Rome. The servicemen included 400 Russians led by a lieutenant colonel. Aid was distributed through Father Dorotheo Bezchctnoff, a Russian priest chosen by Monsignor O' Flaherty. The father was assisted by two Russian women who had formerly worked for the Red Cross.

The original transit flat owned by Mrs Henrietta Chevalier was raided, but a friend forewarned the family. Five POWs were hastily evacuated before the arrival of the SS. The lady suspected that Fascist neighbours might have denounced her. She told the Germans that there had been a few strangers in the building, but they had all gone next door. The troops spent half an hour turning the adjacent flat upside down in a vain search for incriminating evidence.

A day or two later the Lucidi's flat was also targeted. Major Fane-Hervey and William Simpson managed to fool the Germans and escape, as we saw in the last chapter. The raiders were looking for Communist sympathisers and Renzo Lucidi and his French stepson, Gerald, were taken away for further questioning at Gestapo Headquarters. The pair were released without charge five days later after the intervention of the 'Free French' diplomats on behalf of the Rome Organisation.

On 14 February, John Furman unexpectedly reappeared in Rome. He was one of the British prisoners who escaped from the German prison train before it crossed the border. Together with Lieutenant JS Johnstone of the Royal Engineers he spent two weeks cycling 200 miles back to base. Furman went to live with a clerk called Romeo Giuliani. His 18-year-old son, Gino, became one of the lieutenant's main helpers, ultimately with disastrous consequences.

Three weeks later the third billeting officer, Joe Pollak, also returned to the capital. He was among a group of prisoners being loaded onto a train at Sulmona when British aircraft bombed the station. The private escaped in the confusion and hitched a lift on a lorry. He made straight for the Via Chelini flat, unaware that it had been raided two days after his own arrest. The owners were in residence, portly Doctor Ubaldo Cipolla, a German agent, and his Russian-born wife. Fortunately for Pollak, the doctor had decided to play a double game and wished to work for friends on both sides. The soldier was speedily reconnected to the escape line.

Following the Ardeatine Caves massacre at the end of March, all Roman men between the ages of 15 and 70 were called up for forced labour on a defence line north of the capital. Two thousand extra German SS men were deployed in the city and, in what Derry described as the worse development, Fascist terror squads were unleashed. As a result of the adverse public reaction, the Rome Organisation gained many new and valuable supporters, not least a spy in the police headquarters.

Through John May, contact was made with an Italian known only by the alias of Giuseppe, who had an office worker friend inside the *Questura*. This was the base of the very German SS and Fascist *Carabinieri* who were targeting escaped prisoners of war and evaders. For a thousand lire a time - around £2 - the pair were willing to supply a copy of the orders of the day to the British. The commands were only published at midday and reached Derry by a roundabout route in the late afternoon. So everything had to be done at the double, as he recalled:

> Orders for raids usually related to a fairly broad area and I had to rush through our card indexes and maps to find if any of our 'cells' were in danger, for with the increasing number of new billets and the sheer number in occupation in the city there was too much detail to be committed to memory. If billets were found to be in danger areas there still remained the physical task of warning the occupants and arranging evacuations. This was complicated by the security precaution that any one messenger should know of no more than a handful of 'cells.' Consequently we sometimes found that to get warnings to four or five billets quite close to each other we had to trace and despatch as many messengers. [4]

The orders did not cover raids undertaken as the result of urgent information, but they did reveal the extent to which past actions had been the result of denunciations rather than mere bad luck and routine checks. In particular the transcripts exposed the treachery of one of Sam Derry's first helpers in Rome, a pseudo priest called Pasqualino Perfetti who had been seized by the Gestapo and tortured. He led the Germans from house to house and at each gave the secret signal on the doorbell to gain admission. By the end of March, 21 prisoners had been recaptured and more than a dozen Italian helpers arrested. On 7 April, another of the informer's contacts was rounded up. This time it was Gino, the young son of John Furman's host, Romeo Giuliani. Under torture, the youth revealed details of another circuit of safe houses. Ten more escapers were arrested, together with an Italian agent and all the helpers. Fortunately, Furman was away from the flat when it was raided by the Fascists. He was attending a birthday party, which owing to the curfew went on all night.

Major Derry's other lieutenant, William Simpson, was less fortunate. As a result of the denunciations, SS troops broke into the flat of two black marketeers of Greek-Italian ancestry who also did odd jobs for the Germans. The troops arrested Lieutenant Simpson and an American captain, Elbert L Dukate. They had been discussing a plan to charter a boat to escape to Allied territory.

John Furman, learned that the Germans had his description down to the last detail of clothing. They knew the places he frequented and had them under observation. The lieutenant changed his appearance. He cut off his moustache, dyed his red hair black and changed the position of his parting.

William Simpson's place in the organisation was taken by his principal assistant, Renzo Lucidi, who gave up his business interests in the film industry. When it was too dangerous for the billeting officers to be seen on the streets, Adrienne Lucidi would deliver money and supplies to the servicemen in hiding. The pair also helped Flight Lieutenant Garrad-Cole evade capture by German troops at this time, as we saw in the last chapter.

The overall figure for escapers and evaders grew by 300 to 3,739 in April, but for the first time the number in the capital fell, owing to recaptures and a new order from Derry: 'No more ex prisoners are to be billeted in Rome. Any arriving in the city will be given financial help and returned to the countryside.' The capital was both expensive and dangerous, it contained only about a twentieth of the servicemen in hiding, yet absorbed a quarter of the expenditure and accounted for three-quarters of losses through recapture.

Eight escapers were shot during April, 40 kilometres north of Rome, 40 others were recaptured, and more than 20 helpers arrested. Sixteen of the prisoners of war were arrested in routine checks. Three were drunk and disorderly.

The transcripts from the *Questura* also revealed that the Germans were sending out agents dressed as priests to entrap fugitives or posing as Allied servicemen needing help.

On 16 March, Brother Robert Pace, a Maltese codenamed Whitebows, was lured to a village on the outskirts of Rome to collect two bogus escapers. He was arrested and taken to the Gestapo headquarters on Via Tasso together with two Italian helpers. The priest was tortured, but did not reveal anything about the organisation. Eventually he was returned to his mother house. The Italians were shot.

In April, two more priests were confined to their religious houses by their superiors: another Maltese, Father Borg, whose alias was Grobb, and Irish Father Madden, who was known as Edmund. The following month a Dutch priest who had worked in the network from the start, Father Anselmo Musters, codenamed Dutchpa, was hauled from the extraterritorial Santa Maria Maggiore basilica by a large squad of uniformed SS. He was tortured in the Gestapo headquarters for three weeks and a fortnight later sent to Germany by train. Father Musters managed to escape in Florence and returned to a newly liberated Rome in June.

During a friendly chat in April, the German Ambassador to the Holy See, Baron von Weizsäcker, told the Swiss Minister that the military authorities were aware of the help his legation was giving to Allied servicemen. If it did not stop the official most implicated would be arrested. Captain Trippi was forced to cease his activities. John Furman took over his role in liasing with messengers from groups in the countryside. The ambassador had added that aid from the Swiss was unnecessary anyway. It was well known that the British Legation financed escapers and evaders so lavishly that they were often to be seen dining at the best restaurants.

Shortly afterwards, the German College was closed to outsiders. At first there was no contact at all with the rest of the organisation. Then the monsignor arranged to meet agents inside Saint Peter's crowded basilica. The enterprising butler John May devised a better solution. He persuaded friends in the Swiss Guard to let him use their guardroom beside the gate to meet a few specified operatives. In this way, May was able to pass on money and instructions, which Lieutenant Furman and the others committed to memory before returning to the city.

The Chevalier family was again targeted, the result of the rampant denunciations. Mrs M, as she was known to the organisation, told Derry that the flat was being watched and to avoid sending prisoners. When two servicemen who had not received the message turned up she told them to flee and evacuated her whole family under the noses of the watching Gestapo agents. Eventually the Chevaliers were sent to a farm on the outskirts of Rome, where they remained until the liberation.

In the closing weeks of the occupation fears grew for the Allied prisoners still in enemy hands. There were no less than 33 recaptured prisoners of war in three prisons: the Gestapo Headquarters, the Regina Coeli and the Forte Boccea. There were also 50 helpers in the Italian section of the Regina Coeli gaol.

There was no news of William Simpson. By a process of elimination the organisation worked out that he must be in the German-controlled wing of the Regina Coeli. The problem was that the lieutenant was using a new alias. A few days before his arrest the monsignor had given him a genuine Vatican identity card which described him as William O' Flynn, an Irish citizen working in the Vatican Library. In his memoir, *A Vatican Lifeline '44*, published in 1995, William Simpson explained:

> I felt there was some point to keeping my real name from the prison rolls as long as possible. So many of John Furman's group of escapers and Italian helpers had been arrested that, from interrogation of the Italians, John's name was well known to the SS, and he correctly suspected that they were out to get him. Since I had known some of his group, it was highly likely that my real name had been spilled too. It was well left out of the record. In the meantime my Irish name was foiling salvage attempts by some brave outside friends. [5]

The would-be rescuers included the lieutenant's last hostess: the famous Italian film actress Flora Volponi, the double agent Ubaldo Cipolla and Count David Yorck von Wartenburg, a German military police sergeant with many friends in the dissident movement. All failed to find a prisoner under the name of William Simpson.

Finally, on 24 May two members of the Fascist SS called at the prison on the instructions of their notorious commander, Pietro Koch. The Allies had finally broken out of the Anzio bridgehead and Koch had made a deal with the man who until then had been his arch enemy in Rome: Monsignor O' Flaherty. In return for the priest placing his wife and mother in a religious house when he departed with the Germans the Fascist had agreed to leave the Allied prisoners in the Regina Coeli instead of their being transported to Germany. O' Flaherty had insisted that as a sign of good faith the commander should first obtain the release of two British prisoners, Lieutenant Simpson and Captain John Armstrong, an officer held captive for nine months. However, once again Simpson refused to own up to his true identity and the envoys were also unable to locate the captain.

On 2 June 1944, Major Derry was in radio contact with the spearhead of the Fifth Army. He was able to inform them that the Germans were abandoning the city and had not mined any of the river bridges. The prisoners were entrusted to Italian guards, who promptly deserted, leaving the doors of the cells unlocked. Members of the Resistance among the captives took over the Regina Coeli gaol and organised the release of the prisoners in batches, first the women and then the Allied prisoners of war. William Simpson finally gained his freedom. But in a final act of barbarism the Germans took one group of captives and executed them on the city outskirts the following day. Among them was the British captain John Armstrong.

The entry of General Mark Clark's Fifth Army into Rome on 4 June brought the nine-month German occupation to an abrupt end. Early next morning, Monsignor O' Flaherty greeted the general in Saint Peter's Square. The encounter is preserved in a famous photograph, which neatly symbolises the union of the sacred and the secular at the moment of victory.

Major Sam Derry at last became an official member of the British Legation to the Holy See. He was appointed temporary Military Attaché, liasing between the minister and Rome Area Command. In his memoir he said of the network:

> By the time of the liberation, the Rome Organisation had on its books the names of 3, 925 escapers and evaders, of whom 1,695 were British, 896 South African, 429 Russian, 425 Greek, 185 American, and the rest from no fewer than 20 different countries. Fewer than 200 were billeted actually in Rome, but of the thousands in the 'country branch' most, by far, were in the rural areas immediately

surrounding the city, scattered in groups varying in size
from 3 to more than 100. [6]

The verdict of the historians of MI 9, MRD Foot and JM
Langley, was: 'Out of the wreck of many hopes there emerged one
shining example of the British genius for making the best of a bad
job: the Rome escape organisation.' [7]

* * *

The capitulation of German and Fascist Forces in Italy came into
effect at 6.30pm on Wednesday, 2 May 1945. It was followed by
the unconditional surrender of all German forces on the following
Tuesday, 8 May, celebrated thereafter as Victory in Europe Day.

NOTES

[1] Sam Derry, *The Rome Escape Line*, p 47.
[2] Ibid., pp 54-5.
[3] Ibid., pp 90-1.
[4] Ibid., p 178.
[5] William Simpson, *A Vatican Lifeline '44*, p 190.
[6] Derry, op. cit., p 228.
[7] MRD Foot and JM Langley, *MI 9 Escape and Evasion 1939-1945*, p 165.

10 AFTER THE BATTLE

At the end of the Second World War, the MI 9 branch of the British War Office published a report entitled 'The Return of Escapers and Evaders up to 30 June 1945: by areas, services and nationalities.' [1] The document covers 35,847 Allied escapers and evaders across the different theatres in which the secret service operated. There are details on 20,519 servicemen, or 57.24 per cent of the total, in the two areas relevant to Italy: 5,143 in Switzerland and 15,376 in Mediterranean West, from which we can deduce:

1] British Commonwealth Escapers:

POWs in Italy at the time of the Armistice	<u>70,000</u>
Escaped to Switzerland	4,852
Escaped to Allied lines	<u>11,776</u>
Total	<u>16,628</u>
Transferred to Germany	<u>53,372</u>

2] American Escapers:

Escaped to Switzerland	24
Escaped to Allied lines	<u>1,052</u>
Total	<u>1,076</u>

3] British Commonwealth Evaders:

Escaped to Switzerland	64
Escaped to Allied lines	<u>134</u>
Total	<u>198</u>

4] American Evaders:

Escaped to Switzerland	203
Escaped to Allied lines	<u>2,414</u>
Total	<u>2,617</u>

The Allies set up awards bureaux to locate wartime helpers across liberated Europe. In Italy the task was entrusted to a commission that grew out of the official British Organisation in Rome for Assisting Allied Escaped Prisoners of War. Sam Derry spoke of 'the debt to those who risked everything to help us,' a liability which was 'incalculable and perhaps never quite repayable.' He recalled:

> The Rome Area Command had scarcely settled in the city before it found itself deluged with appeals from Italians bearing promises of monetary payment, commendations for good service, and IOUs on odd scraps of paper signed by British servicemen. The Rome Organisation had never issued chits of this sort, but many individual escapers had given them to Italians who had helped them.
>
> It was, I think, a great advantage for the Rome Area Command to know that there was a unit to which the flood of chits could be diverted, and one that could deal with the steady stream of complaints from Italians who had been forced into hiding and now wished to give information against collaborators. To our headquarters were diverted also the hundreds of Italians who, immediately after the liberation, began to besiege Monsignor O' Flaherty's office with appeals for some form of recognition that they had been good patriots.
>
> The key to the truth of most of these claims still lay buried in the Vatican gardens, so, as unobtrusively as we had planted them, we unearthed the biscuit tins containing the records of eight incredible months, and in our new task the bits and pieces of information that had been crammed into these tins proved to be buried treasure indeed. [2]

In October 1944, the overall head of the Rome Escape Line, Sir D' Arcy Osborne, the British Minister to the Holy See, wrote:

> I take this opportunity to record my admiration for, and gratitude to the numberless Italians, mostly of the poorest peasant class in the country districts, who displayed boundless generosity and kindness to our men over a long and trying period. It must be remembered that in so doing not only did they refuse the financial rewards for the denunciation of British prisoners of war which the Germans

offered and which would have been a fortune to them, but they also showed magnificent sacrifice and courage in sharing their few clothes and scanty food and, above all, in risking their lives and the lives of their families and friends in disregarding the increasingly severe German injunctions against harbouring or helping British prisoners. A number of these Italians indeed were shot by the Germans. We owe a debt to the Italian people in this respect that should not be forgotten and cannot be repaid.

Before leaving to become Governor-General of Canada in 1946, Field Marshal Alexander said:

The gallant efforts of these countless helpers resulted in the safe and early return of thousands of our men to their homeland and families, and in many cases soon afterwards to further service with the armed forces. I know I am speaking on their behalf when I say they would all wish, if it were practicable, to thank their helpers personally and endeavour in some way to repay the debts which they have incurred. It is however my intention that due recognition be awarded and all material debts be repaid to every individual civilian who has rendered assistance of whatever nature to Allied escapers. I am glad to say that this immense task is already in hand.

The Allied Screening Commission (ASC) was created on 11 July 1944, only five weeks after the liberation of Rome. It was part of A Force, the Allied deception and escape organisation. The ASC was responsible 'for giving recognition to, and compensating, persons in Italy who had assisted Allied personnel behind enemy lines following the Allied Armistice with Italy on 3 September 1943.'

The Allied Screening Commission was consolidated with its sister A Force organisation, IS 9, to form ASC (Italy) on 20 July 1945. This was abolished on 10 April 1947. Its residual functions were transferred to a newly established Prisoner of War Claims Commission. It was itself dissolved on 31 October of the same year.

The commission's first commanding officer was William Simpson of the Rome Organisation. His successor in October 1945 was Lieutenant Colonel Hugo De Burgh, DSO, OBE, MC, the

Senior British Officer at PG 49 Fontanellato, who had escaped to Switzerland over Monte Rosa at the end of September 1943.

The agency distributed forms to communes throughout the peninsula and processed the consequent claims. The replies were cross-referenced with top secret information obtained as the result of debriefings of escapers and evaders by MI 9 and MIS-X. William Simpson noted that 'false claims were rare.'

Over 75,000 certificates of thanks were awarded at public ceremonies in towns and villages across Italy. There were also cash reimbursements of expenses incurred - for food, lodging and clothing supplied, money advanced, and general unspecified assistance.

The documents were signed in facsimile, most by Field Marshal Alexander - hence their popular name of 'Alexander Certificates' - and the rest by General Joseph Taggart McNarney, Commanding General of United States Armed Forces in the European Theatre. The awards were limited to one per household, so the true number of helpers was far higher.

The Screening Commission operated for almost four years, but within months of its dissolution in the spring of 1947 one of its most important initiatives was swept aside. The British Government and establishment blocked recommendations of British honours and awards for especially deserving Italian helpers. This was despite the signing of the Peace Treaty between the two nations and the pleas of the British Ambassador, Sir Noel Charles.

Together with the other Allied secret services operating in Fascist Italy, MI 9 had made 443 proposals for specific decorations. They included a new honour that was primarily intended for those who had assisted escapers and evaders in enemy-occupied territory. The King's Medal was introduced on 23 August 1945 to recognise courage or service by foreign citizens in the Cause of Freedom. The suggestions for honours and awards to Italian nationals came to nothing.

William Simpson, who had left the Army at the end of May 1946, recalled the successful arguments put forward by the Foreign Office for not implementing the recommendations:

Awards of decorations to Italians would give offence to British families bereaved at Italian hands; some might be Communists; if some were awarded, reaction by others could be counter-productive. And the War Office constituency at MI 9 was gone - Colonel Sam Derry and Lieutenant Colonel John Furman had been released and the Screening Commission dissolved. [3]

In contrast, the Americans awarded Italian nationals 17 Medals of Freedom, 3 for outstanding service. The first British honour to a wartime Italian helper was finally made in 2005. In June the OBE was presented to retired General Daniele Bucchioni in Rome by the British Ambassador, Sir Ivor Roberts. He cited the valuable help that the Italian had given to British and other Allied prisoners of war as a young partisan leader in upper Tuscany. Among those present at the ceremony was Brian Gordon Lett, the Chairman of the Monte San Martino Trust and son of the general's wartime associate, Major Gordon Lett, DSO.

* * *

For a generation after the end of the war, escape and evasion records were withheld from the public on the grounds of national security. The documents are now fully accessible in the national archives.

In 1948, the records of the Allied Screening Commission were transferred to the United States at the request of General Eisenhower. This was despite the fact that probably only a few thousand certificates were issued in respect of assistance to American servicemen in Italy. The claim summaries on individual Italian helpers are still held by the Federal National Archives and Records Administration at College Park in Maryland, reference Record Group 331.

British escape and evasion reports in the names of individual British and Commonwealth servicemen are retained in the National Archives at Kew, reference WO 208. There are also the reports on conditions and events at various POW camps made by neutral inspectors of the International Committee of the Red Cross (ICRC) or the Protecting Power, main reference WO 224.

Further information on the majority of the prisoners of war in Italy who were later transported to camps in Germany or German-occupied territories may be found in completed Liberated Prisoner of War Interrogation Questionnaires, reference WO 344, and in three alphabetical registers kept in the Library and Resource Centre.

In addition, the ICRC headquarters in Geneva holds the records of its wartime Central Agency for Prisoners of War.

Searches are made as a result of written enquiries and an hourly fee is usually charged.

* * *

The French author and philosopher Albert Camus wrote in the wartime underground newspaper *Combat:* 'A people who want to live free do not wait for someone to bring their freedom. They take it. In so doing, they help themselves as well as those who would come to their aid.'

In Fascist Italy, as well as in the rest of German-occupied Europe, helping escaped Allied prisoners of war and downed airmen was one of the earliest and purest forms of resistance.

There were 26,190 British Commonwealth servicemen in the MI 9 global Return of Escapers and Evaders. The secret service's commander, Brigadier Norman Crockatt, DSO, MC, said: 'It can be fairly claimed that of these 90 per cent of evaders and 33 per cent of escapers were brought out as a result of MI 9 organisation and activities.'

Almost two thirds of the successful escapers and evaders, 16, 826 in total, were from the two areas associated with escape from German-occupied Italy, namely Switzerland and Mediterranean West.

Applying the percentages to this figure gives 5,721 British Commonwealth servicemen saved mainly as the result of official rescue work. This leaves 11,105 others who received decisive help from Italian civilians or members of the Resistance. What counted most was the kindness of strangers.

NOTES

[1] TNA: PRO AIR 40/1897.
[2] Sam Derry, *The Rome Escape Line*, p 238.
[3] William Simpson, *A Vatican Lifeline ' 44*, p 222.

BIBLIOGRAPHY

Baio, MC, *Le vere origini della Resistenza Piacentina*, Piacenza: TEP Gallarati, 1976.

Churchill, WS, *The Second World War, Volume V, Closing the Ring*, London: Penguin Books, 1985.

Clifton, G, *The Happy Hunted*, London: Panther Books, 1955.

Comyn, JA, *Episodes*, private circulation, 1994.

Derry, S, *The Rome Escape Line*, London: Harrap, 1960.

English, I, (ed.), *Home by Christmas?* Privately published, 1997.

Farran, R, *Winged Dagger, Adventures on Special Service*, London: Cassell, 1998.

Foot, MRD, and Langley, JM, *MI 9 Escape and Evasion 1939-1945*, London: The Bodley Head, 1979.

Gallegos, A, *From Capri into Oblivion*, London: Hodder and Stoughton, 1959.

Hood, S, *Carlino*, Manchester: The Carcanet Press, 1985.

La Rosa, A, *Storia della Resistenza nel Piacentino*, Piacenza: Amm. Provinciale, 1958.

Lamb, R, *War in Italy, 1943-1945, A Brutal Story*, London: Penguin Books, 1995.

Lett, G, *Rossano (An Adventure of the Italian Resistance)*, London: Hodder and Stoughton, 1955. Republished by Brian Gordon Lett, 2001.

Macintosh, C, *From Cloak to Dagger, an SOE Agent in Italy 1943-1945*, London: William Kimber, 1982.

Mander, d' A, *Mander's March on Rome*, Gloucester: Alan Sutton Publishing, 1987.

Mason, WW, *Official History of New Zealand in the Second World War 1939-45: Prisoners of War*, Wellington: Department of Internal Affairs, 1954.

Merrick, KA, *Flights of the Forgotten: Special Duties Operations in World War Two*, London: Arms and Armour Press, 1989.

Minardi, M, *L' Orizzonte del Campo*, Fidenza: Casa Editrice Mattioli, 1995.

Sbodio, L, *Fornovo Taro nel Movimento Partigiano*, Parma: Step, 1965.

Simpson, W, *A Vatican Lifeline ' 44*, London: Leo Cooper, 1995.

Tudor, M, *British Prisoners of War in Italy: Paths to Freedom*, Newtown: Emilia Publishing, 2000.

Tudor, M, *Escape from Italy, 1943-45, Allied Escapers and Helpers in Fascist Italy*, Newtown: Emilia Publishing, 2003.

Tudor, M, *Special Force: SOE and the Italian Resistance 1943-1945*, Newtown: Emilia Publishing, 2004.
Wilson, P, *The War Behind the Wire*, Barnsley: Leo Cooper, 2000.

INDEX OF NAMES

Guido, Farmer 21-2

Hands, Soldier 124
Happle, S.A. escaper 32
Hastings, S, Sir 90
Haw, N and R 32-3
Hedley, C 49, 51-2
Henderson, Major 41
Hindson, E 106, 108
Hitler, A 115
Holland, C 44-5
Hood, S 106, 108
Hope, H 54-6
Hornsby, D 55

Ines, Civilian 77
Inzani, P (Aquila Nera) 97-8
'Iride,' Helper 124
Ismay, General 39

Jacovides, C (Mario) 99-101
John, S.A. soldier 20
Johnston, JE 15
Johnstone, JS 126

Kane-Burman, M 101-2, 108-9, 111, 124
Kappler, H 124-5
Kesselring, Field Marshal 45, 101
Kiernan, Mrs. 123
Killby, JK iii
Knox-Davies, Soldier 124
Koch, P 130

Laing, A 105-9
Lanza, D 85
Lascaris, G 49
Leng, C 40-1
Lett, BG 137
Lett, G 36-42, 79, 91, 94, 137
Lino, Helper 65

Lockett, V 93
Lockwood, G 37
Losco, A (John) 18
Losena, U 120
Losini, L, Don 76-8
Lucidi, A and R 111, 123, 126, 128
Lumia, G 42

Macaulay, D 105, 108-9, 124
Macintosh, C 35, 38, 40, 91
Mackenzie, AD (Mak) 89, 93, 98
Madden, F. (Edmund) 129
Mainwaring, H 47, 49
Maiocchi, Don 85
Mallaby, R 2-3
Mander, d'Arcy 79-81, 108-9, 124
Maria, Helper 65
Masini, Civilian 82-3, 87
May, J 116, 119, 127, 129
McKee, J 18
McLean, Naval rating 101-4
McNarney, JT 136
Medici Castiglioni, C 72, 75-6
Meletiou, T (Mario) 120
Merli, Partisan 93
Messina, General 74
Meyers, CT 35
Micallef, J 38, 75
Mihailović, General 24, 27
Milic, D (Montinegrino) 88-9, 92
Molinari, GM (Gianmaria) 89, 97-8
Montgomery, General 47, 55
Montgomery, H 122
Moritz, G 19
Moro, L 33
Morton, D, Sir 40